I SURVIVED
RUMBULI

I SURVIVED RUMBULI

by FRIDA MICHELSON

Translated from the Russian
and edited by Wolf Goodman

HOLOCAUST LIBRARY

An imprint of the
UNITED STATES HOLOCAUST MEMORIAL MUSEUM
WASHINGTON, D.C.

Originally published in Russian under the title *I Survived Rumbuli*, © 1973 by Beth Lohamei Hagettaot, Israel. The work was revised and republished by Wolf Goodman, in collaboration with the author, in 1979. This reprint is published by the United States Holocaust Memorial Museum, 100 Raoul Wallenberg Place, SW, Washington, D.C. 20024-2126.

Library of Congress Catalog Card Number: 81-81518
ISBN: 0-89604-030-5 Paper

Printed in the United States of America

Table of Contents

LATVIA

U.S.S.R.

ESTHONIA

POLAND

LITHUANIA

Gulf of Riga

BALTIC SEA

Abrenes

VILAKA
rajons
ZILUPE
LUDZA
KARSAVA
ZILUPE
REZEKNE
DAGDA
MALTA
VILANI
KRASLAVA
BALVI
GULBENE
PREILI
GRIVA
ALUKSNE
VARAKLANI
DAUGAVPILS
APE
CESVAINE
LIVANI
ILUKSTE
SMILTENE
JAUNPIEBALGA
KRUSTPILS
AKNISTE
Gaujenes
MADONA
rajons
GAUJA R.
VALKA
GAUJA R.
ERGLI
JEKABPILS
PLAVINAS
NERETA
CESIS
SIGULDA
ERGLI
DAUGAVA R.
RUJIENA
VALMIERA
OGRE
JAUNJELGAVA
DAUGAVA R.
ALOJA
LIMBAZI
SAULKRASTI
RIGA
BALDONE
BAUSKA
JELGAVA
LIELUPE
ELEJA
AUCE
TUKUMS
DOBELE
SABILE
KANDAVA
SALDUS
AS-MAKA
TALSI
DUNDAGA
KULDIGA
SKRUNDA
VENTA R.
PILTENE
VENTSPILS
ALSUNGA
AIZPUTE
PRIEKULE
GROBINA
LIEPAJA
VENTA R.

Foreword to the Russian Edition

The bloody massacres of the Jewish population of Riga, Latvia, started at the beginning of December 1941. These mass executions took place near the pits of the Rumbuli forest. Only by miracle two Jewish women survived — Frida Frid (later Mrs. Michelson) and Ella Medaliye. From the witness reports of Michelson and Medaliye it is known that after the bloody slaughter in Riga, where during a few days, over thirty thousand people perished, four more escaped — an unknown young boy and three women. (Mrs. Michelson writes about the boy in her notes.) All four, however, perished in the end.

Thanks to the accounts of these two women, the monstrous carnage perpetrated by the Germans and Latvians upon the defenseless Jewish population of Riga in the Rumbuli forest became known. This is why the notes and reminiscences of Frida are of such great interest. They are the only eyewitness accounts.

Upon the liberation of Riga in 1944 a "State Extraordinary Commission" was formed. The objective of this Commission was to investigate the barbarisms perpetrated by the Germans and their Latvian helpers during their occupation of the Latvian territory from 1941 to 1944. In November, 1944, Frida gave testimony of the Nazi brutalities to this State Extraordinary Commission. This testimony, among others, was later used by the Tribunal Courts as incriminating evidence with which to charge the Hitlerite war criminals during the Riga trials of 1946. This evidence was also included in the materials of the Nuremberg trials of the top Nazi criminals.

For years many people appealed to Frida to write down her experiences of her escape and hiding out through the years of the Nazi occupation, particularly about the acts of heroism of people who, at the risk of their own lives, extended her a helping hand and about how she made her own way from the brink of death towards a new life. For years she could not make herself do it — it hurt too much . . .

In 1965 she finally started making notes in Yiddish. Her late husband, Mordekhai Michelson, added some details. He, too, lived through the horrors of the ghetto and concentration camps. This book was put together from these notes.

Riga, Latvia, 1967

*   *   *

Five years have passed since Frida Michelson and I finished writing the book in the Soviet Union that we were hoping to publish. It never saw the light of day there. The book was typed, mimeographed and clandestinely distributed. It was transmitted secretly from person to person through many cities of the Soviet Union. It kindled memories of pain in many hearts, and turned to a sense of responsibility for the fate of our Jewish people decimated by the terrible catastrophe.

At the end of 1971, Frida Michelson migrated to Israel with her two sons.

Let this book of true fact find a way to the hearts of the readers and to the hearts of all those to whom the fate of the Jewish nation is dear — its past, present and future.

David S. Zilberman

Haifa, Israel, 1972

8

Foreword
to the English Translation

On October 5, 1973 my wife and I made our first visit to Tel Aviv, Israel, to visit my father who had settled there in 1971. It was a joyous occasion, for my brother and his wife from Durban, South Africa, were also there. It was a family reunion for Yom Kippur and the Jewish holidays.

In the evening there was the traditional Jewish family dinner to begin the Yom Kippur fast. We went to the synagogue to take part in the service. We spent the next day in the synagogue at prayers and fasting. At about noon we heard a number of cars drive up and stop with a screech of brakes, shocking everyone on this day of days, Yom Kippur! A number of armed men in military uniform entered the synagogue. They went from person to person, speaking briefly, and soon the people folded their Tallith (prayer shawl), and hurriedly left the building. Egypt, Jordan, and Syria had attacked Israel.

Days filled with anxiety followed, everyone close to a radio, air-raid sirens wailing, many hours spent in air-raid shelters, nightly blackouts. At this time my father gave me a book to read, written by our cousin, Frida Frid Michelson, then living in Haifa. The book so fascinated me that I decided to translate it into English and see it published.

Of course I had known Frida before, since we both came from Riga. There she had been a well-known women's fashion designer. We saw each other frequently until 1937 when I migrated to the United States.

With difficulty I found a one-armed cabdriver to take me to Haifa (most vehicles had been requisitioned for military purposes). Frida and I spent three days together, in and out of the air-raid shelter. She talked of her experiences and I took notes. We agreed that an English-language book should be an expansion of the Russian original, which had been written in Soviet Latvia in a guarded style with the hope of publication in mind. In the English work I wished to tell everything, detailing fully all the events and adding dialogue to Frida's story.

It was not until three years later, upon my retirement, that I was able to devote full time to this engrossing project.

Wolf Goodman

Mountain View, Calif.
July 1978

Monument on the site of the Massacre in Rumbuli Forest

Here is the silence of the grave. Death. Night. Eternity.

Rumbuli-Riga, Bikernieki, Salaspils, Klooga, Ponary, Babi Yar, Maidanek, Treblinka, Auschwitz ... Thousands and thousands of cities and towns stained with blood.

I rise from among you, my silent martyrs, old men, babies, fathers and mothers, husbands and wives, brothers and sisters, brides and grooms, children, youths. You were slaughtered by the millions, and you ordered me to tell the living of what happened. I hear your cries and screams, the thousands-strong thunder of your feet running to the grave, your last word:

"R e m e m b e r!"

I s w e a r by the memory of you, by your blood which slaked cruel spaces, by your ashes scattered over the world, by the smoke of your bodies rising from the crematoriums:

I s w e a r t o y o u:

I will tell them, the living, everything — everything that I saw — who killed you and who betrayed you. I will not permit anyone to slander you or say it was someone else. I was with you at the executioner's block till the last minute. Your blood flows in my veins, and your ashes throb in my heart.

I swear to tell the T r u t h, nothing but the T r u t h.

Frida Michelson

1. The Beginning of the Tragedy

It was a warm sunny day in Riga that Sunday, June 22, 1941. I felt like laughing and singing. The sky seemed a deeper blue, foliage a denser green, the birds were chirping louder. Maybe it was just me in a happy mood. Our mother was coming for a visit.

Our mother lived in Livani with her husband, our stepfather. I hardly remember my father; he had died of tuberculosis when we were still small children and lived in Gulbene. My mother remarried after many years of struggling to bring up six children.

"We should take Mama to Bulduri — she has never seen the sea. Fresh sea air and sunshine will do her good."

I was talking to my sisters, Sarah and Neha. The three of us were preparing the table for our guest.

"I think Kemeri would be better," Neha disagreed, as usual. "There she can take the sulfur baths. That should help her rheumatism. Sarah could stay with her while we come to visit on weekends."

"How long would you think she should stay there?" Sarah asked. "I'd think one week would be plenty. We ought to take her to see the city of Riga. She has never been here before. We can take her to the Jewish theater . . ."

"She will enjoy that."

". . . and to the cinema," Sarah continued. "They don't have the cinema in Livani."

"We'd better ask Mama what she would like to do. Let us suggest to her and she will tell us what she would like best."

13

We rambled on like this while setting the table with kosher cold cuts, egg breads and rolls, sponge and chocolate cake, honey bread rich in nuts, butter and ginger (*lekach*), flat squares of white bread made with eggs and sprinkled with sugar and dried to a crisp (*kichlach*), grated black radish cooked in boiling honey and ginger (*eingemachts*), cubes of egg-rich dough cooked in boiling honey, spiced with ginger and sprinkled with poppy seeds (*teiglach*). We had invited friends to meet our mother.

We dressed in a hurry though it was still an hour and a half before her train time. As usual, I changed dresses several times before I finally found something I liked. A little make-up (not too much, Mother may not approve), light white sandals, and I was ready.

Now to help Sarah with her long hair and to tear Neha away from the mirror, and we were on our way. Down the stairs, across the inner court yard, and into the street.

"Let's walk," I said, "It is still forty-five minutes until train time."

"Yah, it isn't too far."

"Only about four kilometers, it won't hurt to walk."

The three of us trotted briskly. Cut across to Marias Iela and straight to the railroad station.

We walked up and down the railroad platform, excitement mounting as the time of the train's arrival approached. No one was talking.

Other people arrived on the platform. A distant whistle, then we could see the smoke as the train came around the bend. With an increasing hissing noise and metallic screeching, the locomotive came to a halt, releasing a big sigh of steam as if it were ready for a rest.

Now came a clanking of doors opening, a rush of

people, porters, conductors, policemen to meet the train. Passengers started pouring out of the cars, pushing suitcases, packages and bundles.

We were looking for Mother. Will I recognize her? It's been over five years! Of course I will.

There, I saw the familiar face. Mother in a dark blue dress, black felt hat, carrying a beat-up old suitcase, was descending the car steps. Her back was hunched, and she looked old and tired after a sleepless night on the train. She looked in all directions searching for us.

"There she is!" I shouted to my sisters. I took off on a run, vaguely aware that I was bumping into people, murmuring apologies. Sarah and Neha were right behind me.

We were hugging and kissing, questioning her about her health, her trip. She was bewildered by this noisy reception. Tears ran down her face (she was always easy on tears), mumbling "All right, all right, all right, children."

She looked sort of sad. I felt that she had something on her mind.

"What is it, Mama? You don't look very happy."

"Children, a strange premonition is tormenting me lately, as though somebody is telling me very bad things are in store for us. Perhaps it is because your stepfather is constantly reading the papers and predicting war. 'Go,' he says, 'go and see your children. This may be your last chance.' So here I am, children. May God keep away from us all the bad things and send us peace, prosperity, good health, and contentment."

"Now, now, stop that crying." Neha was drying Mother's tears with a handkerchief. "It is a happy occasion. Let's be happy and enjoy it."

"There is not going to be a war," I was reassuring her as we started toward the station exit. "The Soviet Union has a nonaggression treaty with Germany. Besides, the Soviet Union is so big and the Red Army so strong that Hitler would not dare attack us."

"I hope you are right. God will be our Protector." Mama was more cheerful.

We were out in the sunshine again. Taxi cabs and droshkies were lined up in two rows in front of the station. The station square was busy with traffic — buses, streetcars, taxis, droshkies, pushcarts, and pedestrians. Mama began to relax as we joined the noisy, colorful medley of the square.

I thought that a slow ride in the droshky would do us all some good. I handed Mama's suitcase to the first driver, up on his high perch. Mama and I sat on the back seat and Sarah and Neha on the front seat facing us. I told the driver to take us to Krišjana Barona Street, 55, by a roundabout way. This would give us a chance to show Mama some of the city sights, catch some sunshine, and breathe some of the morning's fresh summer air.

"There is the other railroad station." I was pointing out to Mama the building to the left, across the square. "And that elevated road is the rail bed that takes you to the seashore, to Liepája and the western foreign countries."

"Why do they need two stations, especially when they are next to one another?"

"There is a reason, Mama," Neha explained. "You see, the Czar insisted on making the distance between the rails wider in Russia than in the rest of Europe when the first Russian railroad was built."

"Why did he do that, just to be different?"

"No, he had good reasons. For one thing, a wider rail bed gives better stability to the train, makes it safer. But the main reason was to forestall the other western countries, Germany in particular, to use their railroad cars and locomotives on Russian rail beds. In case of war, this would be a hindrance to the attacker. In the last World War this proved to be true, even though it did not slow down the Germans very much."

"Where did you get so smart?" Sarah asked.

"Oh, I happened to read about it in the paper the other day."

"And this big brick building on the edge of the square is the prefecture."

"What is the prefecture?"

"This is the main police department of the city of Riga. I was there once to register my passport during the old Latvian regime. And here next to the prefecture is the opera, that large tall white building with the columns. This is a park intersected by a canal. One can take small boat rides over there." I pointed to a dock surrounded by a flotilla of colorful rowboats.

We rode for about an hour, passing the main post office flanked by the high radio antenna tower, the magnificent Brivibas Boulevard, until we turned on Krišjana Barona Street and stopped at the No. 55 apartment building. Mama still looked tired but relaxed by now, and her face had lost its tenseness.

We paid the driver, took the bag, and started through the inner court and up the four flights of stairs to our apartment.

When Mama saw the table laden with all the good food, she exclaimed "All that for me! All that for me!" followed by a gush of tears.

"Yes, it's for you, Mama, and for us, too. Some

17

friends are going to drop by later this evening, and it will be enough for them, too. You needn't cry. Be happy. We are all together. Let's sit down and have a bite to eat."

"I would like to see the rest of the apartment."

We went on a tour.

"Good, good," she murmured, stroking the furniture approvingly as she passed from room to room.

"Now you must all find nice boys, get married, and have children."

"It will come, Mama, it will come," Neha put an arm around her. "All in good time. You don't buy it in a store."

Finally we sat down at the table to eat. All of us were hungry. The spicy meats and the egg rolls washed down with hot tea tasted heavenly. We laughed and joked and reminisced about the primitive life in Gulbene. After Mama went through tasting all the sweets, she was truly happy and relaxed.

"Now, Mama, you lie down for a while and catch up on your sleep," I said. "We have a busy evening ahead. Many friends are coming to meet you, so have a good rest."

To my surprise she did not resist. I pulled the bedspread off Sarah's bed. She took her shoes off and lay down in her clothes without removing her glasses. She gave a great sigh and in seconds was asleep. I closed the door behind me and joined Sarah and Neha.

"How does Mama look to you?"

"Oh, she looks her age, maybe a little better than her age. Let her rest and then we'll see."

"Who is coming tonight?"

The Bobrovs, Chaim Levin, the Sandlers, the Kagans, Ania Sverdlov, your boy friend, Neha?"

"Yeh, he'll probably come later."

"You know, girls, we have no chocolates or any kind of candy on the table," I observed. "I'd better go down to the store and buy some."

"And while you're at it, buy some hard candy, too," Neha said.

I took my handbag and ran quickly out the door. As soon as I reached the street, I felt something was wrong. Up and down the block many people were standing in groups talking agitatedly and arguing. I joined one group to find out what was going on.

"I don't believe it. He wouldn't dare."

"He dared before."

"Yes, but these were small, defenseless countries."

"Holland, Belgium, France — all of Western Europe was neither small nor defenseless."

"I tell you it is just rumor, or maybe a ploy of some kind."

"No rumor. I heard it myself on the radio. Hitler crossed the border on a broad front."

"For once he will get his face slapped."

"Soviet Russia is not Western Europe. We are prepared and numerous."

"This time he is going to choke on what he has bitten off."

"But this means war. No matter what the outcome, we'll all suffer."

It finally penetrated — WAR! I was stunned, petrified, numbed as though I had been hit over the head. War. Before my eyes pictures started flashing — of long-forgotten memories of the past war when I was still a child. Those unending streams of marching soldiers, the trains of horse-drawn artillery and other vehicles, the hordes of refugees, the hunger, the dirt, the lice, the typhoid . . .

War — it will be a long and hard war, an upheaval of our lives, and it could even be the end, the end of all our hopes, of life itself.

I turned and ran back home to report the terrible news. My appearance must have told my sisters that something was wrong for they both exclaimed together, "What is that matter?"

"War. Hitler has attacked the Soviet Union!"

"It can't be" was all they could say.

"Let's turn on the radio," Neha said as we started recovering from the shock. We heard boastful speeches by Soviet leaders: "We are going to hurl back the Nazi hordes," calls to patriotism, reassurances against panic, we are strong enough to withstand the Nazi attack, mixed with war songs and martial music.

Mama woke and stood at the door listening. She understood what we were hearing and tears ran down her face though her expression did not change.

"This is what your stepfather was predicting. It will be the end of us all."

"Don't talk like this, Mama," I said. "You heard what they said on the radio; they said that we are falling back to prepared positions, after the first onslaught, and we will hold firm there."

I really believed what I was saying.

There was no party for Mama that evening. Our friends called to say that in view of the situation they had better not leave home. We stayed close to the radio, hungering for more news. The troubled hours dragged on. We rarely left the house. The news stories on the radio and in the papers were contradictory and did not convey confidence in the military situation. The frequent exhortations to remain calm, that "we have the situation well in hand," had the opposite effect.

Two days later, on June 24 in the afternoon, a formation of about thirty German bombers appeared in the skies over the city. We heard the muffled sounds of the first exploding bombs somewhere far away, and the staccato of the anti-aircraft guns. None of the planes was hit. The sirens were wailing and the radio was repeating: "Air raid. Air raid! Go to your shelters. Go to your shelters."

A loud ring of the doorbell jarred our taut nerves. It was the janitor.

"Everyone must go to the basement. Air raid," he said, and went on to the next door.

What kind of refuge is this air-raid shelter, I thought to myself. If a bomb hits the building, we'll all be buried as in a tomb. We went down to the basement. It was already full of people — standing room only. The basement had been built to serve as a utility room for the building. It was full of boilers and pipes and valves. Hot, stuffy, noisy. People were discussing the military situation. Some had fear in their eyes, but in others I could have sworn I could discern some kind of glee, some kind of malevolent joy. Only later did I find out how right I was.

On the way upstairs after the "all clear," Mama said, "I think I should go back home as soon as possible."

"But you just got here." Neha was indignant. "The front is far, far away. The Germans just want to scare us, demoralize us. It is about time somebody stood up to them, and we'll show them that we can do it."

"Where did you get such a fighting spirit?"

"You ought to listen more to what they say on the radio, and read the newspapers. You all make it out as though we are lost," Neha was angry, but nobody contradicted her.

Back in the apartment we tried to persuade Mama to stay a few days more, but she was adamant.

"In times like these I have to be with my husband," Mama argued. "He is like a baby without me. He doesn't know how to boil a glass of water for tea. Our neighbors were kind to ask him to eat with them. But, no, children, I have to go. I have seen you; you are all in good health, making good livings, and you have your own lives to lead. I hope God sends you good husbands. I am worried about mine and he'll be worried about me."

The next day, with heavy hearts we took Mama to the train station. What a difference these few days had made! Here we had met Mama full of hope and happiness, and now . . .

"Who knows if we'll ever see each other again," Mama said, crying. "Where or when, if ever. It feels as if the ground is blazing under my feet. God bless you and keep you, children. Write when you can."

We led her into a crowded train car and barely found a seat for her. It seemed that many more people than usual were traveling these days.

We walked home silently, each absorbed in our own thoughts.

"I've decided to go to Varaklani," I announced when we reached home.

"Why Varaklani?" Sarah asked.

"Because Varaklani is 500 kilometers to the east of Riga. Because I think that the Red Army is strong enough to stop the Germans far enough away from Varaklani. Because we have relatives in Varaklani. Any more reasons?"

"I think I'll stick it out here," Neha said. "I doubt the Germans will ever get close to Riga."

"I'll stay here with Neha," Sarah contributed.

"What about the air raids?" I asked. "Even if the Germans don't reach Riga, they certainly can lay waste the city, with bombs. I don't think they will get as far as Varaklani or bother with a little town of 1,000 population."

"I have had enough of little towns with outhouses, kerosene lamps and candles, and carrying water from the well," Neha said.

We argued for some time, but I could not persuade them. In the end I said, "If the front gets too close, run east as far as you can go." And I started packing.

2. Varaklani

I was on the train. It seemed that many people had the same idea. I made it as far as the platform of the car. The train was so full that a person standing would have been supported by the crowd. People were hanging on the steps like it was a crowded streetcar, and some said there were people on the roof. Both doors were open and remained so, because it was impossible to close them.

The train left the outskirts of Riga. One could hear the changing of rails pretty often, then the monotonous ta-ta-ta, ta-ta-ta clanking of the wheels on the rails as the train got out on the straightaway. We picked up speed, and fresh air alternating with smoke from the locomotive came in through the open doors. I was surrounded by a sea of faces — gloomy, sullen, morose. No one spoke. Occasionally one could hear the muffled cry of a child, or the train whistle above the clanking of the rails.

Once in a while the train would stop at a station, but nobody got off and nobody boarded.

After an hour or so I felt pain in my thigh caused by the crowd pressing my small suitcase against me. I tried to change my position — not a chance. Suddenly I felt something in my eye, something blown in by the wind. I asked my neighbors to give me room to raise my arm so I could remove the object in my eye.

"If I move, miss, then somebody is going to fall off the steps. Wait until Krustpils, then maybe some people will get off."

My eye was burning but I was helpless to relieve it.

In about two more hours we heard the calls for Krustpils. The train gradually slowed down, then a sudden lurch, and it stopped. I thought my rib cage was broken. Most of the passengers left the train here. There were empty seats! I immediately started taking care of my eye with a handkerchief, removing a black cinder.

The car was half full. I found a partition with only one other passenger, a woman. I took a seat opposite her by the window. The station platform outside was full. People were sitting in what looked like family groups, on their suitcases and bundles. Others were milling around.

"This is where they change for Daugavpils (Dvinsk) or to Zilupe to go on to Russia," my neighbor was starting a conversation. "How far are you going?"

"To Stirniene," I said shortly. I didn't feel like talking. She understood, and we both sat quietly looking out the window. I was trying to put my thoughts in order, reliving the events of the last few days. Have I really done the right thing to run off to Varaklani? Wasn't it selfish of me to leave Neha and Sarah to fend for themselves? What will happen to us Jews if the Germans do take over Latvia? There are plenty of underground *Perkonkrustnik* (Latvian Fascist organization). They'll have a ball.

After what seemed a long time, our train started moving without an announcement. It gradually gained speed and left the crowded Krustpils platform behind. Two or three more hours to Stirniene.

My neighbor took out a wicker basket from under the seat. She unpacked sandwiches, tomatoes, and cucumbers, and started to eat. "Would you care to have a sandwich?" she asked. "You must be hungry — it is almost four o'clock."

25

I wasn't hungry until I started smelling and seeing the food spread out on the opposite seat. Sliced ham was sticking out from the sandwiches. Of course I never ate pork.

"Thank you, I am not very hungry," I lied. "Maybe I'll have a cookie."

I took two cookies and munched them with pretended casualness.

"I am going to Rezekne. That's as far as this train goes." My neighbor again attempted conversation. "My daughter's husband has a farm about twenty kilometers from Rezekne. He is a Lačplēsis* and was given land after the War. I think I'll be safer there, what with all the talk about war." She kept on talking. I was only half listening.

". . . they have two lovely boys, and she is already pregnant again. She wants a girl. My son works in a radio factory. They have a big apartment in Riga with a separate room for me . . .

"He died three days after he came back from the war. Typhus. Typhus, that's what it was. Went through the whole war without a scratch, comes home and dies of typhus. Burned up in three days. We had three fine children, we did . . ."

The train started slowing down and it came to a stop with a jerk. "STIRNIENE" I read on a board on top of a red brick building. I grabbed my suitcase and barely made it down the steps when the train started to move again.

Stirniene consisted of one red brick building alone out in the fields. Several passengers got off as the train went on its way. Varaklani was about eight

* Literally, a man who tears a bear apart. This was the name given to people who fought for the liberation of Latvia in 1918-1920 after the First World War.

kilometers to the south. Two droshky drivers were soliciting passengers for the trip to Varaklani by picking up suitcases or packages. I selected the least aggressive driver. I was his only passenger. He led me to his dilapidated droshky drawn by a sad looking little horse. I remembered someone saying something about a glue factory.

We were the first to pull out of the station yard for I was the lone passenger and I had no luggage to tie down. I sat beside the driver.

"My name is Noah," the driver said in Yiddish. "Noah Silievich. You are a stranger. Who are you visiting?"

"The Talvinskys on Barkavas Street," I shouted above the noise from the iron wheel tires on the rocks of the road.

"Yah, I know them. You a relative?"

"A niece."

"Where are you coming from?"

"Riga."

"I hear they bombed up there?"

"Yah."

"You came to stay?"

"Yah."

The road was full of ruts, rocks, and loose dirt. It seemed that the carriage had no springs. I was sure my insides were coming loose. My driver began to whip his horse to keep from being overtaken by the other droshky, which had three passengers and baggage and a strong horse. After a while the other droshky pulled up even with us and now both drivers were whipping their horses. I held on for dear life, praying that the carriage would not fall apart.

"Stop! Stop!" I shouted. "I can't take this!"

Noah grudgingly laid down his whip, and the horse

slowed down to a walk. The other droshky soon disappeared in a cloud of dust. Noah was hurt, his professional pride injured.

"You city folks are pretty soft," he commented. He said no more during the rest of the trip. The horse plodded so slowly that it had to be reminded by the whip once in a while. I settled down to the monotony of the ride. We were passing meadows, grain ripening in the fields, forests, here and there a farmhouse. The peaceful scene calmed my apprehensions and worries.

It was about 8 o'clock that evening when the irregularity of the road changed suddenly to a regular clip-clop, clip-clop. We were riding on cobblestones. This was Varaklani.

My aunt Talvinsky and her family — my cousins Moishe, Rochele and Dobele — were glad to see me though I had come without warning. But our joy was shortlived.

Only a few days had passed when we suddenly heard a distant roar, coming closer rapidly — Hitler's bombers! People ran out into the streets with eyes raised to the sky. There were two groupings of black specks in the sky. They droned past to the east without dropping bombs. The people, mostly Jews, returned to their work. Nobody spoke, but one could see and feel a sudden change in mood. Heads were lowered, backs were bent.

I knew well what was on their minds: Where are our forces, our planes? Was it all boast and bluster, those reassurances blared out of the radio? Is everything lost? What do we do now? What do I do?

The serenity of the little town was shattered.

"What was all the noise about?" my aunt asked.

"Many planes were flying over and everybody is scared," Rochele answered.

28

"We should have left last Sunday when Motl Gutman left with his family," my aunt complained. "I hear the Germans are hard on the Jews, worse than in the Czar's time."

My cousin Moishe came in. "There is a lot of noise coming from the main road. Sounds like a lot of traffic."

We all ran to the highway. The whole town population lined both sides of the road. There was dust and smoke in the air. Every few minutes a truck packed with Soviet soldiers rumbled by. Then later in the day the trucks started passing more often until there was a continuous stream of traffic, all heading east! These were mostly open trucks packed with soldiers, unshaven, tired men. Sometimes there were closed ambulances, artillery pieces, and passenger cars mixed among the army trucks. Later still, soldiers started coming on foot. They weren't marching like soldiers in formation. They looked like a mass of olive drab humanity laden with packs and rifles (some using the rifles to help them to walk). It was a pitiful sight — our victorious armies.

Some thoughtful townspeople brought buckets of water and tin cups. Every once in a while a soldier would stop for a drink. Questioned about what was going on, the answer was usually a curt "We are running," or "We are retreating."

Oh, my God, it has happened! The impossible, the improbable has happened. All the promises about the strength of the Red Army, about realignment, stabilization of the front, about strategic retreat, these were all lies, empty boasts. What shall we do, what shall we do?

Soon we saw civilians, mostly Jews, mixed with the "Great Russian Might," fleeing to the east. The civilians looked even more pathetic than the military.

Whole families were crowded into trucks, some in horse-drawn wagons, and even pushcarts drawn by men.

I asked some of the people where they came from, where they were going. Nobody gave straight answers, as if everybody had a secret to hide.

We came home in the evening in a very glum mood. There was the one question on everybody's mind, What shall we do? Shall we run, too?

We started packing frantically — deciding and changing our minds as to what to take along. My aunt wanted to take everything and was stopped only by Moishe's repeated statement: "We have only one horse, one wagon, three women, and I'll walk."

There was a steady rumble of heavy equipment from the highway, the tramp of feet and the clank of iron tires on the cobblestones all night. We slept little. At three the next morning it was light and we got up.

I ran to the highway. It was almost quiet and empty. Only a few straggling soldiers tiredly dragging their guns. It was clear that the front was near. They were the last ones. The Germans were close. We have to run. I ran back to the house with panic in my heart.

Apparently others had the same idea. People were throwing things into their wagons. Some were taking off with the horses on a dead run, the whips snapping in the air.

Moishe had the horse and wagon waiting in front of the house. We were all sitting in the wagon. My aunt was saying goodbye to the neighbors.

"If you are running, run to Russia," one said. "If you run to hide in the villages, they'll rob you and kill you. I don't trust the Latvians."

"Where will you go?" another old lady was trying to dissuade her. "We are old people, we don't harm anybody, they will leave us alone. Don't panic."

1934   1934, Kemeri Beach

Frida Michelson at the Rumbuli Monument

A young girl came by. "We were running by train and reached Zilupe but not one of the crowd of refugees was allowed to cross the border into Russia. Here we are back. We don't know what else to do."

There we sat in the wagon listening. My aunt was confused, as we all were. She didn't want to leave her neighbors, friends, house and goods; but we were also scared of the Germans and the Latvians. We still remembered the atrocities of 1919 after the occupation of Varaklani when the Latvian soldiers were given thirty minutes to do as they pleased. Murder, rape, and robbery reigned for those thirty unforgettable minutes. Many widows, fingers chopped off for the golden wedding rings, and many bastards with blond hair and blue eyes were left as living memorials.

A man came by. After listening a while, he spoke up: "It is too late to travel by horse and wagon. The Soviets have gone and the Germans are not here yet. I hear that the local population has all the roads under fire. It is too late to go anywhere."

Moishe lost his patience. Without a word he pulled on the reins and directed the horse away from the people.

We turned off the main road and reached a large log farmhouse. We were met by a huge dog, barking fiercely. Then he recognized Moishe, quieted down and started wagging his tail. A tall blond man followed by a heavy-set woman with a child in her arms appeared in the doorway.

Moishe patted the dog and walked up to the porch. He shook hands with the man and warmly greeted the woman. They talked for a while, then all three approached the wagon.

"We can stay with Alex for a while until it quiets down in town," Moishe announced in Yiddish.

We were introduced to our benefactors, Alex and

his wife. They spoke a typical Latgalian dialect with many Russian words thrown in.

"You speak like a West Latvian. Are you really Jewish?" Alex asked me.

"Yes, I am Jewish," I said. "I live in Riga, and that is how they speak up there."

"You can stay with us for a while," Alex said, "until things settle down. I owe that much to Moishe, my friend, for the many times we stayed at your house when we came for Sunday church."

"We'll bed you down in our new barn," Yadviga, Alex's wife, spoke up. "There is new hay so it will be soft and you'll be comfortable."

We slept fully clothed so it took a while until the fleas got to us. I scratched and struggled until I was exhausted. I finally gave up to the little bloodsuckers and fell into an uneasy sleep.

We were up with the roosters and out of the barn to explore the yard. Alex joined us, then Yadviga, nodding to us, went to the stable to milk the cows.

We saw a man coming out of the neighboring forest. He was very tall and broadshouldered. He had red hair and his face was red also. He was about 20 years old and dressed in a rough linen shirt and pants and birch bark shoes tied with strings. He took Alex aside and they talked in whispers, looking at us once in a while.

Alex came back to us. "This fellow says that you can go back home. It is quiet in town. Nobody will hurt you."

The whole thing looked suspicious to us and we were frightened. Alex sensed this and said, "I'll go to town myself and find out." He turned and left with the young man.

In a couple of hours Alex returned alone. We were all standing with a question in our eyes.

"Don't be afraid, everything is peaceful and quiet in town," he said as he approached. "I think you should return right away before bands of robbers form and attack you on the road."

We left after a hurried meal. My aunt gave Yadviga some money and her face lit up.

We came to Varaklani without incident. It was indeed quiet and peaceful; too quiet and too peaceful, as before a storm.

Next day the first Germans appeared in town. The word went around that these troops had landed by parachute. They found no opposition. On the contrary, many local Latvians were leading them around and showing them where Jews lived. They went into Jewish houses demanding food and sometimes removing jewelry from the owners. They were very arrogant, but no violence was reported the first day. The soldiers started a systematic requisitioning of butter, eggs, milk, bread, and other products.

One German soldier came by our water well with a canvas bucket. Before he drew water, he called us out of the house and warned:

"If the water is poisoned and if only one German soldier suffers, then hundreds of Jews will be destroyed."

My cousin Rochele and I were lying on the grass in front of the house the same afternoon. The sun was shining — it was warm but not hot. Rochele had her arms around me. I was enjoying the closeness and affection of the child. I closed my eyes and tried to relax from the strain of the last few days.

"Fräulein! Fräulein!" We were up in a second. A German soldier was calling, coming toward us weaving a crooked course — drunk. Rochele stood behind me and held onto my hand. She was shaking.

"Fräulein, sind sie zum haben? [Are you to be

33

had?]" he asked when he came near. He took off his hat and made an exaggerated bow that nearly toppled him. Rochele held me tight and I felt her shivering behind me. With great effort I tried to keep calm.

"You see there, the two-story brick building?" I said pointing toward the building about half a kilometer away. "They have several beautiful fräuleins who will accommodate you very nicely, I am sure."

"Danke schön." He saluted, turned, and staggered off in the direction I had pointed out.

"To the attic!" Rochele shouted, and we ran as fast as we could. We were scared, but at the same time we felt good about the trick we had played. Through the attic window we watched the German soldier go into the red brick house. Soon he was out shouting and shooting his gun in the air. He started to look for us, knocking at several doors. We were shaking with fright. Luckily he did not remember which house had given him the wrong information. He finally quieted down and walked away.

Later the same day we saw a local Latvian, accompanied by a German officer, pointing toward a field of rye behind our house. A little later several armed German soldiers, rifles at the ready, waded through the shoulder-high rye. They flushed out about a dozen Russian soldiers. The Russians looked dirty, tired, and bedraggled. The Germans pushed them along with their rifle butts. This kind of scene we saw repeated for several days. Many groups of prisoners were driven out of town, shots were heard. There were rumors that many wounded and sick had been shot. Our hearts ached for those prisoners. There was a question in our minds we didn't voice: Does a fate like this await us too?

Several days later, large posters were put up all

34

over town, in both German and Latvian languages. It decreed that Jews were prohibited from associating with Gentiles. This included treatment by Gentile doctors, use of "Aryan" servants, staying in the same line with them, etc. From here on Jews could buy food only in a specially-designated store in the marketplace.

As the stored staples at home dwindled, the lines at the "Special Store" grew longer and longer. The supplies in the store were of poor quality and scant. Many times the supply was exhausted before half the people could be served. The doors would close and many would return home with empty baskets. We got the idea — slow, gradual starvation. Then people would come to the store hours before the doors opened to secure early places in line. Arguments would break out over a place lost in line, over being pushed, over stepping on toes. Any real or imagined pretext provoked quarrels and irritated frayed nerves. Germans passing by and other local "Aryans" would stop and laugh at what went on in the line. The spectacle became a source of amusement to the local "Aryan" populace.

One time a girl of about 19 or 20 stood in line. She was mentally retarded and could not control her facial features. She appeared to be making faces and laughing for no reason. Some passing German soldiers stopped and watched her behavior. They took her out of the line and demanded that she sing and dance for them. She refused. They mercilessly beat her with their short leather riding crops. The girl screamed in terror while the Germans bent double with laughter.

Every day the Germans rounded up some Jews, primarily older people, and organized work details.

They were made to clean streets and public buildings much more thoroughly than necessary. It was clear that this was done to insult and humiliate.

The German soldiers organized requisition parties. They would select a prosperous Jewish house and requisition all the food they could find. They would stuff their pockets with silver, jewelry, and anything else they fancied. Once in a while they would take along young Jewish girls to their headquarters. There they raped them, beat them, and threw them out the second-story windows.

To make themselves as unattractive as possible, the Jewish girls stopped washing and combing their hair. They wore dirty old clothes.

These are the events of the first days of the Nazi occupation in Varaklani.

One day an official bulletin was plastered all over town and in the neighboring villages. It invited all the peasants of the Varaklani district to come to the marketplace on the following Sunday.

I dressed in peasant clothes to prevent recognition and went, too. The crowd was enormous. Standing on the hill by the mausoleum, I could see the whole marketplace below. The square was full of people, horses, wagons, with still more streaming in from all the side streets. In the middle stood a newly built wooden platform. German officers in full parade uniform, bedecked with medals, stood on the platform; loudspeakers facing in all directions. Armed German soldiers surrounded the platform.

At exactly 10 o'clock in the morning came the now familiar, "Achtung! Achtung!" The crowd was still milling around but settling down.

"Achtung! Achtung!" was repeated a few moments later. The crowd fell silent, all heads turned expectantly toward the platform.

"Achtung! Achtung! Der Herr Oberkommandant of this area is here to convey greetings from our Führer Adolf Hitler, to our Latvian Aryan brothers. After we have distributed presents to you in an act of friendship, Der Herr Oberkommandant himself will speak to you. You are free to enter the Jewish homes and help yourself to what was plundered from you for years by the Jews. It is yours!"

Suddenly the Germans started throwing into the crowd straight from the wagons various items, mostly sundries: packs of cigarettes, matches, coffee, spools of thread, etc. The air resounded with shouts, screams, and squeals. People were pushing, fighting over cigarettes, watches, spools of thread. The mob was trampling people underfoot. The platform toppled over and the officers with it. Shots were fired in the air to quiet the crowd, to no avail. The mob was out of control. "They are shooting at us! They are shooting at us! Run! Run!"

That afternoon we were sitting in the house. Nobody spoke. Nobody ventured outside. There was a strange silence all over town.

Suddenly we heard knocking on doors and loud voices. We ran to the windows. We saw local policemen knocking on Jewish doors, then whole families driven out. They came to our door: "All Jews are directed to assemble at the marketplace. Take your brooms and spades with you." Then to the next house.

"They are going to kill us," my aunt was crying. "You, Rochele, hide in the cellar and the rest will go."

"No, I am afraid to be alone."

"I don't think they'll harm us," I said. "They probably want us to clean up the mess they made this morning in the marketplace. You see they are not counting the people, not even escorting us."

I guessed correctly. All the Jews were assembled at the edge of the marketplace. Armed German soldiers divided us into details of ten and set us to cleaning up the place.

The wounded must have been carted away earlier (there were rumors that they numbered more than a hundred). Several hundred people spread out over the marketplace, sweeping, scrubbing, scraping the debris from the ground. A big bonfire was started under the direction of the soldiers. Into it we threw broken boxes, damaged merchandise, cloth, anything flammable, We dug a deep hole and pitched in bottles, metallic objects, and the like. By nightfall we had the marketplace clean as it had never been clean before.

We were called together and told to go home and not venture into the streets until 5 o'clock in the morning. Those who did would be shot.

Rumors started circulating that all the Jews were going to be killed. Latvians — acquaintances, friends, neighbors — quit talking to us. When we met on the street, heads turned away. It was as if we already did not exist. Old friendships vanished. We felt from all these signs that death must be near. We were tormented by a fear which gradually turned into a kind of numbness. It was hard to concentrate on anything. Every knock on the door frightened us, every strange voice. We were afraid they were coming for us.

We decided that when they did come, we would take poison. My aunt had some rat poison and distributed several tablets to all of us. We were so sure of the approaching end that we slaughtered all the chickens, scratched up the furniture, tore up the wall paper, poured ink on the living-room rug, and did all kinds of damage to the household so the Germans or Latvians would never enjoy it. Several days passed in this mood.

On July 15 a rumor swept the town that all the refugees who had come to Varaklani were to be allowed to return home. I went to the police station to confirm this.

"You may travel wherever you want," the policeman at the desk said in an unfriendly manner.

"Could you issue me some kind of document, permitting me to travel to Riga?" I asked, showing him my passport.

"We don't give permits and don't guarantee that you'll get where you want to go," he said sternly.

That was that. I decided right then to go back to Riga. Now the problem was how to get to the railroad station in Stirniene, eight kilometers away. I went to a Gentile carrier.

"Mr. Ozolin, I am a refugee from Riga and I was told by the police that I can return now. Take me to Stirniene. I will pay you whatever you ask."

"Look, Miss, I am not even supposed to talk to you, a Jewess, much less drive you to Stirniene," he said in a low voice. "I could take your money, kill you, and dump you out somewhere on the road and nobody would punish me. I am a poor man, but I am an honorable, Godfearing man.

The Jewish driver Noah lived on the outskirts of town. I went there, my bag in hand, taking the back streets. I was dressed inconspicuously, but clean and well. A dark gray suit, no jewelry, no makeup, black stockings and shoes, a deep hat to hide my hair and face as much a possible. I thought I could pass for a Latvian provincial young lady.

Noah started talking before I could say a word: "I

39

am not going to take you, miss. I have a wife and children. They'll shoot us both on the road."

"I have to get to Riga, Noah," I pleaded. "You dress like a peasant in linen pants and shirt, a big straw hat, go barefoot. Drive your wagon instead of the droshky and nobody is going to recognize us as Jews. I'll give you four times your pay."

Noah looked up at his wife in the door of the kitchen, and shook his head: "No."

I finally found another Jewish driver and in the afternoon we were on the road to Stirniene. The wagon had no springs. The sacks of hay we sat on were not much help. I guess the human body was made to take all kinds of punishment. After a while I got used to the knocks and shakes and I relaxed. We met several military cars going in either direction. They paid us no attention — we were local yokels.

A lot of Jewish people were waiting for the train on the Stirniene platform. They sat in family groups, men, women and children, apart from the Gentiles. Probably refugees like myself.

"How did you get here?" I tried to start a conversation with one family.

"The same as you," was the evasive reply.

I understood. Nobody wanted to talk. One does not know to whom he is talking.

Soon the train arrived. The people ran to the different cars. It wasn't crowded, plenty of room. I chose a compartment occupied by only Latvian women. As soon as I sat down on the hard bench the train started moving and gathering speed.

I could see two Jewish women going into the next compartment. They looked like a mother and daughter. The mother cried and sobbed without letup. She was lamenting — apparently a near relative had been killed. Her daughter was trying to console her. Their Latvian fellow travelers grumbled. They were annoyed by the continuous sobbing and lamenting. "The damn Jews," they mumbled and moved over to our compartment.

Toward evening the train came to Krustpils. It was announced that the train would go no further. A train for Riga was promised for tomorrow. Most of the passengers stayed in the car; I didn't go out either.

Time was dragging on. Lively conversations were going on all around me.

I happened to look through the window. There before the ticket office of the station was a long line of Jewish people. They were being registered. I recognized some that I had seen at the station in Stirniene. The question of what it all meant tormented me. I left the car and started walking nonchalantly on the platform along the train. I wanted to have a better look at what was going on at the ticket office. One woman signalled me frantically with her eyes not to come near. I barely acknowledged the message and, looking past her, I continued on my walk.

One of my neighbors in our compartment met me walking in the opposite direction, stopped and said in a low voice: "Guess what I just saw," and without waiting for an answer continued, "I just saw a whole bunch of Jews driven into a freight car; then they locked it and nailed it over with boards."

She turned and walked in my direction. "There," she said, pointing to a red freight car on a siding. It was nailed over with many boards along the seams and the door.

"One hundred eighty-three Juden" was written in chalk in two places.

She immediately spread the news to the rest of the

passengers as soon as we reached our compartment. Of course, I was the corroborating witness.

In the compartment I was taking part in the conversation — I was accepted. Gradually the conversation died down. I feigned tiredness and pretended to sleep. The rest of them followed suit.

But I did not sleep all night. The thought that there were people in that sealed freight car did not leave my mind. "Juden, 183 Juden," the chalk markings stood before my eyes, burning me inside. There could only be that many people if they were standing. What fate awaited them? They'll suffocate; they'll die in there. My conscience started gnawing. Why am I here masquerading as a Gentile while my fellow Jews are dying in agony? Is it right for me to do what I am doing; don't I become a part of the society that is perpetrating all this; don't I myself become a tormentor of my own kind? Somebody must survive; somebody must, in order to carry on my own kind, to tell them what is happening. I am a witness. I must survive as a witness. Is it perhaps that God has chosen me to be the witness, and others like me? No, I must do everything I can, except betrayal, to survive; I must fight for my survival.

The idea that somehow God had chosen me to be His witness sustained me throughout the whole ordeal and was instrumental in my fight for existence when submission and death would have been so much easier.

The dawn was breaking. A bright reddish sun came over the horizon, but in my heart was darkness and despondency. One by one the passengers began to waken and go to wash and freshen up.

Some of the passengers were leaving the car and walking toward the green lawn behind the railroad station. I followed, trying not to become separated from my neighbors. Somehow I felt protected by them. We stretched out on the soft grass. It felt good after the hard bench we had slept on all night. My neighbors opened food sacks, ate, drank, and talked. I dared not open my own food for that would have given me away. I was offered some salt pork and bread — "Don't you have any food?"

"No, " I replied, "I didn't think it would take so long . . . Thanks, this tastes very good," I said, choking (I had never tasted pork before). After a few bites it did taste good — I was very hungry.

One woman took out a deck of cards. "Anybody know how to read cards?"

"I think I can," I said on an impulse. "I once read a book called 'Cards Don't Lie,' written by a Gypsy." This was not really true, but I had once seen a Gypsy reading cards. All of a sudden I became the center of attention. They spread out a large shawl on the grass, handed me a deck of cards, and sat down around me. Women from neighboring groups joined us. I was sorry I had started it. With this much attention, someone might expose me. Too late. I had to go on.

"What would you like to know?" I asked the middle-aged matron to my right who had given me some sweets earlier.

"About my husband, is he alive? Where is he?"

"Tell me the color of your husband's hair and eyes."

"His hair is gray now, but it used to be blond. The eyes are blue."

"That would be the king of hearts," I was sort of talking to myself. Finding the king of hearts, I put him in the middle.

"Now, shuffle the cards, then close your eyes and

think hard about your husband. Then at random pull out three cards while your eyes are still closed, and hand them to me."

My imagination was working hard to put on this act. I hoped it would work. I put the three cards face down on the king of hearts. I divided the rest of the cards in about four even bundles and placed one on each of the four sides of the king of hearts, talking all the time: "This is on top of his head, the future; this is under his feet, the past; this is on his left hand, the present, near his heart; this on his right hand, the present, on money."

I lifted the three cards from the king of hearts saying, "This on his heart and mind. Oh, the queen of hearts! With the six of clubs and the eight of hearts. He is thinking a lot about a fair-haired lady who is related to him and also about his home."

"That must be me!" she shouted, elated. "Tell me, is he alive?"

"Yes, he is alive," I said in a slow monotone as though in a trance. "He is now in some kind of federal enterprise, or employ, or institution."

"He is in the army!" she shouted. "Oh, dearie, how did you know? You are telling the truth. Tell more."

"He had an accident, or maybe he was wounded, but not seriously at all. He didn't even go to a hospital. He is all right. There is a lady, you see the queen of spades. Watch out for her. She is telling lies about you."

"His mother!" she squealed. "Oh, you know so much."

So it went the whole morning. I was choosing clients whom I had overheard talking so I knew something about them. More and more I gained assurance of myself. I was making everybody happy by saying good things, mixed with a little not so good to make it more believable. I was the star of the group. Some of the women cried upon hearing the good news and wanted to give me money but I refused.

At about one o'clock the train for Riga was announced. We hurriedly changed to different cars. Most people kept to the same groups, as I did to mine. I was invited to have the place by the window because of my popularity and mastery of the cards.

The whistle sounded, the locomotive roared, and the train started to move. We were finally on the way to Riga. The monotonous sound of the wheels on the rails, the swaying motion of the car, and the sleepless night must have overridden my resolution to stay awake.

Somebody was waking me, "My dear, you must be having a terrible nightmare," my neighbor was saying. "You were moaning and groaning."

"What did I say?" I was awake immediately.

"You were saying 'Don't, don't' as though somebody was hitting you."

I noticed a man standing in the doorway staring at me. I felt he suspected me of being Jewish. When our eyes met, I felt a piercing, cold feeling envelop me, there was so much hate and evil. Now he will expose me and this will be the end. I collected myself and started to talk animatedly to my lady neighbors.

"Thank you for waking me. I don't know what came over me. I never nap in the daytime."

"Would you like a bite to eat?" inquired the lady whose husband I had brought back to life. "I have to preserve my figure," I said. "I design clothes to order for wealthy women, and I have to model my own clothes."

"See that you don't overdo it," she cautioned.

"Some people get sick from not eating enough, you know."

"No, I don't intend to be a pretty corpse yet," I joked. "My grandmother was always telling a story about a farmer who bragged how he taught his horse to get along without food, and if he hadn't died he would have taught him to get along without water, too. I remember this story and won't let that happen to me."

Everybody laughed. Even my suspicious observer's face softened with a smile. He turned and sat down facing away from us. Must be that my perfect Latvian and my unconcerned behavior convinced him that I was a true blue-blood "Aryan," despite my dark complexion, black hair and eyes. I started breathing easier.

The train stopped at a station called Gostini. From the direction of Riga came a long train consisting of open-platform cars. On the platforms were hundreds of young Latvian volunteers. They were dressed in the gray-green uniform of the old Ulmanis* home guard army, their belts weighed down with all kinds of armament. I heard them shouting:

"Are there any Jews in your car?"

The panic returned. I could see myself being dragged off the train and pushed into a boxcar destined for death.

"No Jews here," this was the passenger who had looked at me so suspiciously. "We are no Jews."

Thank God, I can breathe again. Our train moved on. In a few hours we were in Riga. I intended to go directly to my apartment.

* The Latvian dictator before the Soviets took over.

46

3. The Riga Prefecture

It was the 16th of July [1941]. I was walking over the familiar streets of Riga. What a change! There used to be many Jewish faces on the street. Now at every step one met the German military in their resplendent uniforms walking in the company of Latvian fräuleins in light dresses, joking, laughing, flirting.

I took a streetcar. There was not a Jew to be seen. Maybe it was prohibited for Jews to ride streetcars? When my street, Krišjana Barona, came I ran up to my apartment. No key. I rang the bell. There was no answer. I went downstairs to the janitor, Kozlovski. His wife met me at the door.

"Do you know anything about my sisters?" I shot out, even before the customary greeting.

"The last time I saw them was before the Germans came," she replied. "They wanted to leave a key with me, but I did not take it. I did not want to have the responsibility."

"Didn't they leave a message for me?"

"No, they did not say anything, what they were going to do or where they were going." She paused for a moment, them added, "If they were trying evacuation, they were probably caught and killed. Terrible things have been going on here."

"My God!" was all I could say. I stood there as if I were nailed to the floor. I felt faint. The janitor's wife took my arm and led me to a chair.

"Take hold of yourself. Many bad things are happening to Jews nowadays. Thank God you are still alive."

Mrs. Kozlovski offered to have me stay overnight. I accepted.

The next morning I decided to go to town to see some of my friends and find out what I could.

"You can leave your suitcase here, it will be safe when you return. Why should you drag it around?" Mrs. Kozlovski said. It seemed logical. I thanked her and left.

As soon as I crossed the street, two armed Latvian policemen with red and white armbands left a building entrance and approached me.

"Ah, we caught the birdie!" they shouted triumphantly. "Let's go!"

"What kind of bird am I? You must be mistaking me for someone else." I was taken dumbfounded by the sudden assault.

"Don't talk, just go," barked one policeman.

They held my arms as though I was trying to escape and dragged me through the streets triumphantly. Contempt was in the eyes of passers-by. We marched to the prefecture, the big red brick building by the railroad station that I had pointed out to my mother just a few short weeks ago.

I was led into a cavernous basement and there they let go of me. There were no formalities of checking or name-taking. The room was crowded with Jews — men, women, young and old.

"Please let me go home," I said to the guard. "I must get some clothes and toilet articles. I have only a summer dress on."

He pushed me away. It was no use, my begging fell on deaf ears. Some mothers were pleading to let them bring their children to breast feed, to call friends to take care of the children — but they might as well have talked to the wall. They were answered with mockery and brutality. There was nothing to do but to accept the situation and just wait for whatever was to come.

I was still eager to know what had happened in Riga in my absence. I could get a clue to the fate of my sisters, perhaps, if I started asking people what they knew.

I heard stories of monstrous villainous atrocities perpetrated on the Jews by the Germans in the first days of their occupation of Riga. Thousands of men and women of all ages were caught and thrown into various prisons. No one knew what happened after that, nobody came back. Jews were caught in the streets, at work, at home especially at night, dragged from bed and sent away, without clothes, food, in underwear — where? Nobody knew.

Special attention was given leaders of Jewish societies — the scientists, physicians, engineers, lawyers, architects, businessmen, manufacturers. When recognized they were removed from the crowd of Jews in detention and shot on the spot. Their Latvian professional colleagues were instrumental in making identification and most of them were pleased with the turn of events.

Thousands of Jews, including children, were caught in the streets and organized into work details to bury the dead, sweep the streets, clean buildings, etc. In many instances they were forced to perform senseless tasks purely for the amusement of the tormentors and the humiliation of the tormented.

The columns of Jews, driven through the city into forced-labor camps or into the trenches where they were mowed down by machine-guns, were subjected to abuse not only by the Latvian police but also by the citizenry — they were pushed, slapped, and spat upon.

The people in work details were forced to labor from sunup to sundown, rain or shine. They were given no food or water, and of course, no pay. Occasionally a few were allowed to go home for the night. They were told to be back the next day, failing which they would be shot. The majority, however, were returned to the basements of the prefecture, to the crush of the cramped quarters, stale air and filth. People could only find a place on the floor and rest as best they could, only to be driven out again to the back-breaking work with the first rays of sunlight.

There were stories about white-bearded old people being forced at the point of guns to put on their Tallith and Tefilin,* and dance and sing Soviet songs. Girls and women were forced to remove their clothes in front of men and perform disgusting sexual acts. At other times women were raped in the presence of their husbands and children by the Latvian police. Many of the women went insane.

The remnants of the Fascist organization, the Perkonkrust,** which remained underground during the Soviet occupation, rose up again with the German invasion, flourishing and expanding. This political party was the source of anti-Semitism during the twenty years of Latvian independence during the time of democratic government. Now with the coming of the Germans they had to outdo the Nazis in cruelty to the Jews who fell into their hands. Their headquarters on 19 Valdemar Street (now Gorki Street) was the center of torture and systematic an-

* Prayer shawl and phylacteries.
** Thundercross (literal translation).

nihilation of the Jewish population of Riga. The Per-konkrusts supplied the anti-Semitic invective through their publications; they formed the organization for mass murders and served as a training school for the executioners. They were given the responsibility for arranging for the disposal of properties of their victims. They far exceeded their Nazi bosses in their barbarism.

I was terror stricken from all these tales. It was hopeless. They brought us here and we would be shot tomorrow. What can I do? Oh, what can be done?

* * *

The troubled hours were dragging on. There was no hope, nothing to look forward to, except death. There were no more words, no tears, no regrets, just a listless passage of that abstract concept of time.

The door suddenly opened. A soldier carrying a binder of papers said, "We need twelve women to work in the fields right away."

He proceeded with the selection. I was among them. Something was very disturbing about this. A white-haired, lean, stooped old lady was also among us. It was rumored that old people were not taken in work details. Their destination was — the pits . . .

They took us in a truck across the River Dvina to a railroad station, Zasulauks. We were told to climb into a freight car and it was locked behind us. In about an hour the train stopped. The car door was opened, we were led out and formed a line. Here we were guarded by policemen. They were writing our names on a list. This was the first good sign, the first indication that we were not going to be shot.

I looked around and recognized where we were — in Yelgava. I knew many people here, but much good could they do me now. There were few civilians on the streets, mostly German military and policemen. As we stood there we saw a group of civilians marched by under police escort. They were not Jews. They must have been people accused of Communist activities. It was common in those days to be accused of "Communist-Jewish" activities by enemies. Their clothes were torn and dirty; they looked tired, an empty look in their eyes. They knew where they were going . . .

After the policeman finished our registration, we were commanded to march. We marched for a long time over dusty roads, hungry, thirsty, and tired. Some of the weaker ones could barely walk. The sun went down behind the forest; it was getting dark. Still we did not know where we were headed. Finally, after about ten kilometers of marching we came to what looked like a rich farm. It was late in the evening.

A middle-aged Latvian with a lantern came out of the house. He spoke to our guard, then told us to climb up a ladder to the attic above the cows' stalls, for the night. We struggled up, one by one. I had to help several women, they were so weak and exhausted. Most of us had had nothing to eat for the last twenty-four hours; we were tormented by thirst and oppressed by fear. What awaits us tomorrow? Do we have a tomorrow?

There was a layer of straw on the attic floor. We piled together close to one another for warmth and were soon asleep.

"Get up! Time to go to work!" a voice interrupted the few hours of rest. It was still dark. We climbed down. A guard was waiting for us and led us to the kitchen.

This was a good sign. They would not feed us if they were going to kill us. We started to live again.

We were taken to our work — weeding acre upon acre of sugar beets. The leaves of the beets could hardly be seen for the weeds.

The soil was loamy, dry and hard. This made it difficult to pull the weeds. We women, city dwellers all, were unused to this kind of work. Pretty soon our hands were covered with bloody scratches and blisters. One could not stop to rest; we were watched constantly. The guard measured a certain plot every morning that we were supposed to clear that day. If we did not, he threatened to shoot us. And it was clear that he could carry out his threat at any time. We had to work very hard to accomplish the daily task.

When the work was finished in one village they took us to another and another. The work was the same. The working day lasted from dawn to dusk. It was forbidden that we wash ourselves or our clothes and these were the only clothes we had. Dirt and sweat had eaten into our bodies so that we itched all the time. Nobody had a comb, so our hair became a haven for lice. There were no breaks in the workday. Only one consolation — they fed us.

Some nights were cold. There was nothing in the way of covers. We heaped together even closer for warmth but this was of little help — we were just freezing together. Few of us could sleep.

From this type of life and work our bodies grew weak. One time the little old lady with us fell over in a faint in the field. We took her aside, stretched her out on the grass, and revived her with cold water. The next day a girl named Bobrova was sunstruck. She vomited and had a bursting headache. We thought she was going to die. We begged the guard to let us take her into the shade, and we promised, of course, that we would do her share of the work. I, too, felt ill once. My head felt dizzy and hurt terribly, and blood spurted out of my nose. I squeezed my nose with a cold, wet rag and stopped the nosebleed, then went back to weeding.

The days dragged on.

Once a different guard, armed with an automatic gun, rode by the field on a bicycle. When he saw us — Jewish women — working, he became hysterical.

"Who dared bring those damn Jewesses here? They'll contaminate anything they touch!" He pointed the automatic weapon in our direction. "Who is in charge here?"

"I am," our guard said, and ran to him waving a paper. "They are performing useful work here by the order of the Riga Commandature."

They exchanged a few angry words and the stranger rode away. Later the farm woman told us that if our guard had not had the paper declaring his responsibility for us, we would all have been shot by the stranger, right there in the field.

The news that "Jew-women" worked in the fields spread around the neighboring villages. The local Fascist toughs banded together and started coming over nightly to our stalls. They shouted obscenities, shot guns in the air, sang dirty songs, and generally acted wildly. The farm owners as well as the guard did not dare interfere with this activity. These nightly goings-on robbed us of our last refuge — sleep, the only time to forget our troubles and renew energy to face another day.

We had a young teacher in our group. She was despondent and ready to give up. "They will drain all our energy first and then kill us. It would be better to kill ourselves now and not let them have the benefit of our work."

"The work is our salvation," I argued. "As long as we can keep on working we'll stay alive. I am all for staying alive."

These kinds of arguments flared up often. I was trying to keep up the spirit of the group. I was convinced that if we could make ourselves useful we would stay alive.

Another problem developed. We had a girl about 18 years old from Kraslava. She would hide in the tall grass and just lie there. This angered me. The rest of us had to do her share of the work in order to complete the day's task. I asked the guard to give each person a separate assignment of work to be completed. He agreed, and that ended the loafing.

I worked hard and fast. After completing my assignment, I usually helped our old lady, and even then I had time left over. The guard allowed those who finished their work to go to the river to wash. This gave me a chance to wash my dress too. I dried it on my body. What a relief that was. And I was finally able to take revenge on the lice.

Thus passed six weeks. We completed the weeding of the sugar beets in the whole area. On the day we had finished, the guard announced: "There is a new decree: All Jews must wear the six-pointed Star of David. It must be made of yellow material and sewed on to your clothes in a prominent place."

We did not have yellow cloth, so we made Stars of David from brown cardboard. Our teacher tore into me: "You see, I was telling you that a bitter end awaits us. Did we need to work our fingers to the bone to be paid with a bullet?"

"I don't think this is the end of us. We demonstrated that we can be useful, therefore they will let us live. Anyway, you haven't lost a thing," I retorted.

After a while the guard led us in formation to the river. There a small tugboat waited for us.

"Now you will see," the teacher started again. "They will take us out a little farther, to the middle of the river, and throw us overboard."

"Don't listen to her, don't give way to panic," I was trying to calm the group. "We worked well and they will let us go home."

The guard ordered us to get in the boat. After we were aboard we cast off and were on our way.

"Where are you taking us?" we asked our guard.

"You'll find out when we get there," came the curt answer.

We felt uneasy. God knew what awaited us. We sat there depressed, waiting any minute for the end . . . The boat kept going, the motor droning monotonously. In a couple of hours we saw on the horizon what looked like the spires of the Riga churches. Joy overtook us, as if there were no Nazis in the city.

The boat came ashore and tied up at the pier. The guard said, "You have all worked very diligently. Now you can all go home."

Home?! We couldn't believe our ears. We fell to kissing each other, even the school teacher, and crying. We parted and went our separate ways.

I decided to go to my apartment in spite of the previous experience. I was hoping to meet my sisters there or even to get some news of their whereabouts, or perhaps by some signs they had left I would know what they did. With this in mind I walked to my apartment. There was a sign on the door in large German letters: BESCHLAGNAHMT [Requisitioned].

So my apartment and everything in it now belonged to the Germans. What now? I decided to go to the prefecture. I went and boldly turned to the Latvian policeman on duty.

"I just returned with a group of Jewish women from work in the fields around Yelgava. We worked there hard and diligently for six weeks. Now I cannot get into my apartment; somebody else lives there. I want to get in and at least take some of my clothes and few belongings. The furniture and the apartment they can use."

The policeman looked at me intensely for a moment. Then he started looking in various books, checking various papers. In the end he said, "Yes, you are right. It checks. You did work very well. Wait here a little while. I have to get rid of these papers and then I will go with you and find out what the trouble is."

He put away some books, filed papers, and was ready to go. Soon we were out on the street. This policeman acted humanely compared to the others. He introduced himself as Svipste and talked to me respectfully. I hadn't experienced such behavior in a long time and was elated.

I brought him to the door of my apartment. He looked at the sign — BESCHLAGNAHMT — and pushed the doorbell long and hard.

A young Latvian woman, about 30, opened the door. She was wearing my black suit (this suit I hold dear as a relic even today).

"Hi, fräulein . . .," the policeman Svipste began inquiringly.

"Krison," she introduced herself.

"Who put up the *Beschlagnahmt* sign?"

"I did."

"On whose authority?"

"Some German officers are my friends. They said I

could have this place. As a matter of fact, I am now the manager of the whole building."

"Why were the German officers so generous with you?"

"I have given them some favors."

The face of the policeman showed just a trace of a smile.

"You have taken the law into your own hands, fräulein Krison. You cannot take over somebody else's property without written permission, even if it does belong to a Jew. Do you have such a permission?"

"No."

"Then you are illegally here and expropriating private property on false pretenses."

"That black suit she has on is also mine," I put in.

Her face flushed, she became confused and embarrassed.

"Let's go in and have a look," the policeman said, inviting me in.

Fräulein Krison wasn't much of a housekeeper. I had never seen my apartment so filthy. Empty bottles, glasses, dishes with leftover food. Cigarette burns in my good sofa and furniture. Cigarette butts ground out on the parquet floor and on my Persian rug. It looked like a good many wild parties had taken place here.

Sarah's bedroom was packed full of boxes of clothes, furs, and shoes. None of these things belonged to me, and I said so. These thing must have been taken from other Jewish apartments.

A little spark of avarice appeared in the eyes of the policeman. For a moment the two adversaries looked at each other: Svipste with greed and envy, Krison with fear and hate.

"Fräulein Krison, you will vacate this apartment today. Don't take a thing that does not belong to you. The black suit you are wearing must be returned to the owner immediately."

To me he said, "You have my permission to live in your apartment. I will send someone over later to remove the things that don't belong to you."

I thanked him. I was afraid to stay in my apartment. Who knew what Krison could do to me. These were far from normal times. I quickly packed a bag with some underwear, a couple of dresses and, yes, my black suit, and an overcoat. And I left without speaking a word to the fräulein.

I couldn't pass up the opportunity and the temptation to ring the doorbell of janitor Kozlovski's apartment. Mrs. Kozlovski opened the door. Her face changed color — first pale, then crimson. She was seeing ghosts. My eyes spoke the hate and accusation I felt. She was perspiring.

"Honest, Miss, I had nothing to do with it. My husband . . . he was told to do it . . . this is the law. They even came and took away your suitcase later." She lied. I knew she lied, she knew she lied, and she knew that I knew. Yet she continued. "We haven't any of your things. Fräulein Krison, that bitch, she lives in your apartment." She caught her breath and was glad to change the subject. "She robbed all the Jewish apartments. All the parties she is having, all the neighbors are complaining. Why should she end up with all the good things and all we get is junk?"

"This is for you to find out," I cut her off, slammed the door and left.

Where could I go? Who will take me in? Sonia Bobrov came to mind. She was one of my best friends. She will not turn me away. I haven't seen her for a long time. She was one of the guests invited to meet Mother.

Sonia Bobrov (née Tager) lived with her husband and young daughter in a house on the corner of Red Army and Avotu Streets. I hastened there, rang the bell, and Sonia stood in the doorway. We fell into each other's arms. I cried to the point of hysteria. Sonia began to worry: "There, there, Frida. Take hold of yourself and tell me all about it."

I finally calmed down and told her everything that had happened to me, both of us crying at times in the telling.

Sonia prepared a bath for me, the first one in so long. Finally, I could comb the tangles out of my long hair. I revived. All the clothes I had worn in the villages had to be thrown away — they were falling apart, some parts looked like leather, they were rotten. What a pleasure it was to sit in the hot bath and use soap, real perfumed soap! All the fears, the dangers, the hardships were melting away . . . It was bliss. Then, to climb into a soft bed between two white sheets, to wear a clean nightgown, and to have an understanding person at your side was luxury — beyond reach and imagination just a few short hours before. How pleasant, how dear, how appreciated the simplest things in life become when one is deprived of them. I could not have valued them before the war.

It was not to last long, though. I asked Sonia: "What happened in Riga while I was gone? How is the situation for the Jews? What can we look forward to?"

"Better go to sleep and get some rest, there is time enough tomorrow."

"No, tell me, tell me all of it. I have to know what's in store for me tomorrow."

"It isn't good and it isn't pretty," she started. "Just about all of our synagogues have been profaned, defiled. You know the Choral Synagogue on Gogol Street. It is no more. The masterpiece of architecture, filled with archaic art treasures — it is no more . . .

"The back yard of the Gogol Synagogue and all its halls were filled with people — men, women, children, oldsters and youngsters — the refugees from Lithuania. The ones who did not escape far enough and fast enough were stranded here and put up camp in the synagogue. One day the Perkonkrusts and other Latvian hangers-on surrounded the synagogue and jammed everybody inside. They piled wood and straw on all sides and set it on fire. My Latvian friends who witnessed this told me that the inhuman cries, shrieks and screams of terror were indescribable. People who tried to break out of the windows were mowed down with automatic weapons and pistols while the onlookers howled and rolled with laughter.

"The same happened with the synagogue on 63 Stolbovaya Street (now Engels Street). They held up setting the fire to it until they brought our beloved and internationally known rabbi Kilov. They pushed him in with his congregation and started the fire . . .

"The old synagogue on Moscow Street . . . There they thought up a different twist in atrocities. The murderers caught every Jew, in the predominantly Jewish neighborhood, and filled the synagogue to capacity. The overflow of Jews who could not get in were forced, under the muzzles of guns, to put wood and straw around the synagogue, pour kerosene on it, and set it on fire. Thus they were forced to burn their own families and kin. When the fire took hold and the tormented screams filled the air, the Perkonkrusts let go with their automatic weapons to get rid of the Jews

61

outside the building. Oh God, will anybody ever know and record it for history — the scenes where flames, shots, blood, screams, and wild drunken laughter were mixed into one . . .

"Other Jewish holy places met the same fate. The Jewish cemeteries were desecrated. In the new cemetery in Shmerli, the Fascists burned down the funeral parlor; the chapel with all the caretakers and their families (Khevra-Kadisha) were burned alive, including the famous Riga cantor and music professor Mintz with his family.

"Even the old cemetery, which hasn't been used for years, did not escape the fire and desecration. There, too, they had driven several hundred Jews into the buildings, and threw hand grenades through the windows.

"Many famous people perished in the carnage. They just happened to be where these bonfires were taking place. Sarah Rashin, the violin virtuoso of European fame, met her end there . . .

"The Jews in the provinces were no better off. The news from the little towns and villages was scarce. It came by chance and in bits and pieces. But one can gather that the Jewish population there was completely exterminated by the local Latvian Fascists under the guidance of the SS bosses. Only in the large cities, like Liepava and Daugavpils did a small number of Jews still survive. Some of my Latvian friends told me that they saw signs saying *Judenrein* (free of Jews) in some smaller cities like Tukuma, Yelgava, Bauska and others.

"Information was scarce. From the first days of the Nazi occupation an invisible wall of isolation was erected around the Jews. It was forbidden for Jews to move from their living places. The Aryans were forbidden all communication with Jews.

"I met a few Jews who were freed from forced-labor camps and brought back from other parts of Latvia. They too were uncommunicative. Could be they were numbed by hurt and despair or just did not want to spread bad news which we had plenty of in Riga, too, or create unnecessary panic."

Listening to all the accounts of these horrors, I asked, "Why do you think they killed all the Jews in the provincial cities and villages but left some Jews alive in the larger cities? Why do you think the Jews of Riga were given preference over the Jews in the provinces?"

After a long pause, Sonia replied: "It could be they fell victim to the wave of pogroms in the first days of July. Many Jews in Riga too were wiped out. It could be that after they satisfied their lust for blood that the rest of us would have a chance? Or . . . it is horrible to think, God in heaven, are we destined to the same fate? Is there no way out?"

I was terror stricken. My mind could not fathom, could not comprehend the viciousness, the inhumanity of man to man in our so-called civilized society. My imagination could not paint the picture of the people before their nightmare death, or feel the pain, the torment of the close ones who were forced to see all this. Was there no end to the boundless suffering?

4. The Ghetto

In the beginning of August a dim ray of hope flashed on the otherwise dark horizon of the Jews in Riga. We started hearing rumors that 30 or 40 physicians and engineers who had been arrested during the first days of the Nazi occupation were freed from the Central Prison. We were hoping that the thousands of other prisoners still alive also would be freed. The stories told by these few liberated, however, checked our hopes. Large groups of prisoners from the Central Prison were being taken somewhere, in a continuous flow, over a period of many days. None returned. From bits of information from the inhabitants of Bikernieki area we finally pieced together their fate. During the month of July many trucks, loaded with people, passed by. Later, uninterrupted firing of machine guns was heard from the direction of the neighboring Bikernieki Forest. The trucks returned empty. Now we knew, without doubt.

"But what did the release of the craftsmen (shoemakers, tailors) and professionals mean?"

"Maybe the Germans need them in the military factories."

"But what about the physicians? It was forbidden for Jewish doctors to treat Aryans, the same as Aryan doctors were forbidden to treat Jews."

"Maybe they were afraid that without medical help epidemics would break out among the Jews and spread to the Aryans. They did announce the opening of an outpatient clinic for Jews on the corner of

Moscow and Livani Streets. The doctors were probably meant to work in this clinic."

Thus we were piecing together fact and rumor and trying to figure out and predict what each occurrence meant.

The means of isolating the Jews from the "Aryan" society was accomplished through the *Judenrat* (Jewish Committee). This was to give it an air of self-determination and self-administration. All communication to the Jewish population went through the Judenrat, consisting of appointed Jewish people. Some members of the Judenrat occasionally tried to intercede to ease the burden of the terrorized Jews, to no avail. It became clear that the Judenrat was a fiction, created to help the Nazis organize the annihilation of the Jewish population.

In a few days I decided to visit my apartment again. I had to find some clue to the disappearance of my sisters. On the way I saw some Jewish people with the yellow Star of David on the chest and on the back. It was odd to see them walking in the street, avoiding sidewalks. I was walking on the sidewalk out of habit. An elderly Jewish man stopped me and started explaining.

"You are probably new here and don't know that it is strongly prohibited for Jews to walk on the sidewalk. You may face grave consequences if someone should report you."

I thanked him and took to the pavement. From here things look differently. One has to walk in the gutter, close to the curb, to avoid being run over by the traffic. Also one feels humiliated, which was no doubt the purpose of the ordinance. This elevates the "Aryans" above the less worthy races of the world of the New Europe.

Jews were walking in single file, like geese. They were marked with the Star of David, which looked like a fall maple leaf stuck on by the wind. It seemed unnatural and perhaps funny, if it hadn't been so tragically real.

I came to the door of my apartment. My ear to the door — quiet. I rang the bell. Fräulein Krison opened the door. She gave me the key according to Policeman Svipste's orders. No words were spoken. She left.

I started looking for indications of what could have happened to my sisters. Sarah's room was cleared of the stolen clothes. There was great disorder all over the house; no sign of attempts to clean up. I found Sarah's and Neha's clothes and some other things, but it seemed to me that they would have taken them along if they had planned to be evacuated. So many Jews disappeared without a trace, I hoped against hope that they were not among them.

I was afraid to remain very long. An idea struck me — why don't I offer my things to some of my Latvian good friends, an inheritance, so to say. Mezhulis — she was one of my best clients for many years. She lived on the other side of the River Dvina.

Mrs. Mezhulis greeted me warmly. I told her of my bitter experiences and proposed that she go to my apartment and come back with some of my clothes and the many pieces of yardage I had there. I described the things, the shapes, the colors, so that she could claim them as her own, as though she had come to pick up these things in view of the fact that I am out of business. She was very happy to take me up on this. She went and obtained from Fräulein Krison everything she asked for.

In a few days I decided to pay another visit to my apartment. However, first I rang the bell of my neighbor Lambert across the hall. We had been good friends in the past. She was quite alarmed and upset when she saw me. She pulled me inside quickly and locked the door.

"They are after you! Last night there was a lot of noise on the stairway, so much that it woke everybody up. We went to see what it was all about. Two men in Perkonkrust uniforms were knocking on your door and threatening to break it down if you didn't open up. When they saw us they shouted that it was none of our business and barked commands to us to go inside — otherwise they would use their pistols on us. Next morning, we found out that they were the brothers of Fräulein Krison. They came to arrest you because you are a Communist. Fräulein Krison was bragging about it to all who would listen, that her brothers are very important people in the new Reich and consequently she too wields a lot of power, and that damn Jewess had better not show her face here again. It was lucky for you that you didn't spend the night here. They would not have let you go free."

It was clear to me that I should not go to my apartment again.

* * *

"All able-bodied Jews must work." This was the curt decree. I must find work. Sonia Bobrov got me a job as a domestic servant to a German officer on the corner of Elizabeth and Umaras Streets.

This officer and his orderly lived in the apartment that belonged to Sonia's brother, Tager. Tager was arrested and shot during the first days of the German occupation. His wife and infant had fled in time. From the whole family, only Sonia's elderly mother was left alive. She had come to live with her. This is how Sonia knew of the officer.

My responsibilities were to clean the apartment, wash clothes and other things that a house servant normally does. The orderly taught me how to do things for his pedantic boss. Everything had to be just so, according to German rules and tastes. It was hard at first until I got used to the routine. No food or pay was given to any working Jew. The compensation was just, so to say, that you got to live another day. Still, I was glad to have this job. Some envied me. It was better than working all day in the open dragging rocks, cleaning streets, and the like.

Once as I was going home from work, a youngster in school uniform approached from the opposite direction. When he came close, he suddenly kicked me in the stomach with great force. I fell backward in the street. I cried, more from humiliation than physical pain. I got up and started complaining to the policeman on the corner.

"Who was it, a Jew?" he asked as though he was ready to intercede.

"What difference does it make?" I said. "This is hooliganism. There, you can see him, he stands at the intersection in a school uniform."

He laughed, "He could have done worse to you. He could have spit in your face or choked you to death — that is his right. He is the boss here."

I was shocked. I was nothing. I was worse than a dog, an insect that can be squashed by anyone, no questions asked.

* * *

My German officer lived happily and contentedly. Latvian girls visited him every day. They locked the door and one could hear laughter and other kinds of noises. The orderly winked at me sometimes. I paid no attention. Once when I came to work in the morning I met at the door three gaily dressed young Latvian girls. When they saw me they all burst out laughing. One of them addressed me:

"The Jewess comes to work. You'll have plenty to do today. Just go in the bathroom." Still laughing, they slammed the door.

I have never seen such filth, such foul muck maliciously perpetrated. I cannot describe it out of respect to the reader's sensitivities. It took great physical and mental effort to cleanse that bathroom so no trace or odor was left.

One day the officer came in disturbed and upset. He said to me, "Fräulein, you and I will have to part company. There is a new decree that requires the dismissal of all Jews that work for 'Aryan' people."

He walked back and forth in the room and talked as though to himself: "It's a pity, it is a great pity, such a good worker, so intelligent. Listen, maybe you are not Jewish at all? Maybe there is just a little 'Aryan' blood in you, huh? Then maybe I could make an effort to keep you. I could say that you are my mistress. What do you say, eh? You are a pretty woman."

"No, no. What are you saying? I am a full-blooded Jewess."

"A pity, a great pity. In that case you will have to leave me; I'll miss you," he said in distress.

So I lost my job. This caused me automatically to lose my *Ausweis* — the permit to go into town. In a few days we found out the reason for this. All Jews were ordered to move to a ghetto in the Moscow Forshtat, a Riga suburb.

Few people understood what the word ghetto meant in those days. It was something abstract, but on everybody's lips.

Sonia and I decided to stay together. We went to

see what the ghetto looked like and try to find a place to live.

We found that they were putting up barbed-wire fence around a rather small area, from Lachplesha Street along Ludzas Street, up to the old Jewish cemetery. This area was a desolate and neglected one, where the poorest population lived. Before it was designated as a ghetto, a few poor Jewish families lived here, but for the most part it was settled by Russian workers and craftsmen. The housing conditions in this area were far inferior to other parts of Riga. Many of the houses lacked plumbing, electricity, toilet facilities, gas or central heating systems. There were many one-story wooden houses, old and dilapidated.

Since non-Jews were forbidden to live side-by-side with Jews, it followed that all the Gentiles were to be resettled — but where? In the areas from which the Jews had been driven out, of course.

It was decreed that only four square meters per person were allowed in the ghetto. About 30,000 people squeezed together in a compound of a few streets. Under these circumstances everyone had to leave behind most of their furniture and clothes. The "Aryans" who took over the evacuated apartments were the big winners.

The Latvian Fascist newspaper *Tevia* described the Warsaw Ghetto in existence for almost two years as a paradise: the Jews have everything there, even a café and a theater. Seeing what went on here, we came to the conclusion that the story must be a lie and a mockery.

Sonia and I were walking the streets of the ghetto. We saw that there was a grocery store. Many Jewish customers were in line. They came from all around the city. This was the only legal place where Jews could buy food. There were few products and what there were were of poor quality. Most shelves were bare. Some people were managing to buy products from "Aryans" illegally of course, at jacked-up prices. If it hadn't been for that, most of us would have starved.

Sonia was very despondent. She had a family — her small daughter and an old mother.

"How are we going to live in the ghetto? Such conditions! Do you think we can take it?"

I was not too sure myself. Many questions tormented me too. However, I tried to console my friend. "Calm down. We aren't the only ones. Somehow we'll settle down here the way other people do. We'll work, help each other and hope . . ."

We finally found a small apartment in the ghetto at 37 Ludzas Street. We moved in a few days later. One bedroom, kitchen, living-dining room, toilet stool — no bath, one sink in the kitchen, a wood-burning stove. It was on the first floor with one window looking out on the street. The window sill will provide entertainment for the old mother.

I managed to make one last trip to my apartment. Fräulein Krison was not home. I took some blankets, linen and clothes, then alerted Mrs. Lambert, my good neighbor, to take any furniture and clothes she wanted while Krison was out.

The ghetto apartment was very dirty. The walls hadn't been painted since the house was built. The wooden floor was badly worn and begging for a mop. Mice, cockroaches, spiders, fleas, and bedbugs — all were in evidence.

Sonia and I worked for several days cleaning and fighting the vermin. The house smelled of kerosene and soap that we used. Somehow we fashioned curtains for the windows, hung some pictures on the walls, put a clean cloth on the table, and it became home.

We had two beds. Mother slept in one, Sonia and I in the other, and Nadienka, Sonia's little girl, on the sofa in the living room. Gradually things settled down to a daily routine. We spent our days standing in line at the ghetto store to purchase fresh food. More time was spent shopping through friendly "Aryans" for canned, smoked, and dried food products. To be sure, we paid almost double the price to compensate for the risk they were taking. We kept our foodstuffs in nooks and crannies throughout the house. This was to protect it from the eyes of jealous and nosy neighbors, and even more from the policemen who would help themselves to anything they pleased on unexpected visits.

People began burying silver, money, and jewelry during the night. This was all done very ingeniously. A deep, slanted hole was dug so that the cache was really beneath a bush or a young tree. The items were placed in a linen sack which in turn was placed in a tin can, then sealed with wax. The hole was then skillfully covered with sod so that no trace of digging was left. Only the owner could unearth the belongings, and very few did. The ghetto grounds became a veritable mine of precious metals and stones in a short time. I wonder what future archeologists will think of their finds.

Every day I watched from the living-room window and saw large formations of men and women passing by on their way to work. They were the work battalions, led by civilian Latvians and German soldiers, to the work places in the city. We did not register for work yet. We were putting it off as long as possible. There was no pay or food for the work.

On October 24, 1941, the installation of all double barbed-wire fencing was completed. The ghetto was now completely cut off from the outside world. On Sadovnik Street was the entrance with a small building for the *Wache* (guards). From this day on free movement from the ghetto to the "Aryan" part of the city was forbidden. The punishment was death.

Drunken SS men in the company of Latvian Perkonkrusts would often come into the ghetto at night and create havoc. Bad luck would befall the person who happened to be outside. He would be beaten and sometimes shot. At times they would break into a house, rob it, beat up the people, and leave with someone. Nothing was ever heard of that person again.

The *Wache* searched the people returning from the city working crews. Anyone found with food products was severely punished by beating and, of course, the food was confiscated. Some were in this way beaten to death, others were shot. Food became even more scarce. The ghetto store had only half rotten apples, potatoes, carrots, beets, and cabbage for sale. No bread, meat, sausages, or herring was available. Most people lived on the products they had squirreled away before the ghetto was closed. The guards did a good business smuggling in products and charging exorbitant prices. Many homes started feeling the pangs of hunger.

As bad luck would have it, the winter of 1941 came early and was severe. It was hard to get wood for heating. People were chopping down the few trees that were there and even burning furniture to keep from freezing.

Hunger and cold — what next?

5. The First "Aktion"

On November 28, 1941 the Germans issued a decree to liquidate the ghetto. The women, children, the elderly, and the ones incapable of working were to be taken to a special camp. The able-bodied men were to stay in a specially fenced area and would be used for work in the city. It was also stated that the people who were to be moved must immediately prepare for the journey. Each person was allowed to take with him no more than 25 kilograms of clothing and food.

This order hit like a thunderclap, creating chaos and panic. Gone were the complacency and relative feeling of safety of the ghetto.

"No sooner do we get established — move again."

"This is our lot — The Wandering Jew."

"Where can they move so many people in such a fierce winter without more clothing and food?"

"How many people will be able to tolerate the trip in such weather?"

"Where are we going?"

"Without fathers, grown sons, without healthy men who could help us."

So the talk went. There was no time to think. The next day, November 29, we were supposed to leave the ghetto and start the trek to the new camp — where, nobody knew. Such was the order.

The whole ghetto was in motion like ants in an anthill. We made and remade packages; we prepared knapsacks, selected and re-selected the more necessary clothing and food, compared lighter things against heavier. We tested the packs for each person for the weight and comfort in carrying them.

Especially tragic was the plight of mothers with infants to carry and small children to lead.

The ghetto lived through a terrible night from Friday the 28th to Saturday morning the 29th of November — the last night before parting with the loved ones — the relatives — fathers, sons, brothers, husbands. The feeling was that this was parting forever. Nobody slept, nobody ate, few words were spoken. By morning no more tears were left to shed and hopelessness set in.

At dawn the able-bodied men were herded together on the corner of Ludzas and Sadovnik Streets. They were formed into columns and left standing there in the cold for hours. At about one o'clock in the afternoon an order came to move the men within half an hour into the *Kasernierungslager*. This was what they called the special area, fenced in with barbed wire inside the ghetto. It was later called the small ghetto. It is hard to describe the terror, the confusion this new order created. Men were running to say their last goodbyes to their loved ones, to leave or take some package of food and try to smuggle younger boys back into the houses. Everybody thought that it was the men who would be liquidated.

We, too, were packing. Many decisions had to be made. We put on several layers of underwear and clothing. I topped it off with a white working smock. We paid special attention to the food. Just the same, we could not take everything we needed even if they were going to resettle us somewhere, and if not . . . we wouldn't need anything anyway.

There was fuss and bustle in every house, with the packing for the move. The richer ones, who still had jewelry and money left unhidden, sewed it into the clothing of the children, or left it under the boards of the floor.

As evening drew nearer the atmosphere was growing more tense. Columns of armed Latvian policemen came marching into the ghetto. Some looked drunk. Here and there we heard shots. As it became darker, the shots became more frequent.

At about seven o'clock in the evening, several policemen ran into our apartment. They shouted orders: "Out, out this minute! Form five in a row with the rest of them."

We were deathly scared. Quickly harnessing ourselves to the knapsacks, we ran outside, not bothering to close the door — we were not coming back.

Ludzas Street was full of people. We mixed in with the rest and formed a column five abreast.

There was a ringing, crackling frost out there that night. Our five people stood shoulder to shoulder to keep warm. Even the smallest whiff of wind was biting to the face and made tears stream from the eyes.

Somewhere, not far away, we heard continuous shooting. We stood there, stamping our feet to keep warm, for about two hours. The policemen disappeared somewhere, perhaps to chase out people from other areas of the ghetto.

We stole back into the house. Many other people followed us into our house because it was close by. Pretty soon our house was filled with people looking for just a little warmth. We kept our heavy clothing on, waiting to be ordered out on the road any minute.

So passed hour after hour. Gradually the exhaustion and fatigue started taking its toll. I have never seen people sleep standing up, but everybody was asleep in whatever position they happened to be.

It was still dark at seven o'clock in the morning. Shouts from the Latvian policemen woke us. "Out, out! Everybody out!" We were rudely wakened to grim reality. The sleepy-faced people piled out into the street again and formed columns five abreast. Several policemen ran up and announced that only the people living on Lachplesha to Daugavpils Streets would leave today. The rest could go home.

We ran back home, happy that we could stay home a little longer and rest from the terrible night. We unhitched our knapsacks, threw the packs on the floor, and started peeling off our clothes, Everyone wanted to rush to bed for rest and warmth.

I went to the window to see what was going on. It was already beginning to get light. An unending column of people, guarded by armed policemen, was passing by. Young women, women with infants in their arms, old women, handicapped, helped by their neighbors, young boys and girls — all marching, marching. Suddenly, in front of our window, a German SS man started firing with an automatic gun point blank into the crowd. People were mowed down by the shots, and fell on the cobblestones. There was confusion in the column. People were trampling over those who had fallen, they were pushing forward, away from the wildly shooting SS man. Some were throwing away their packs so they could run faster. The Latvian policemen were shouting "Faster! Faster!" and lashing whips over the heads of the crowd.

I started screaming uncontrollably: "They shoot the Jews! They shoot the Jews! Come see the nightmare!"

I scared everybody out of bed. One by one they came to the window. Somehow they managed to quiet me down: "Get away from the window," they urged. "They'll notice you and start shooting at you, too."

I stood there as if I were nailed down. I couldn't move — it was as if some mysterious force kept me there, paralyzed. My mind was aflame: "You must see it. You are the witness. Take it all in. There, before your window, before your eyes the tragedy of your whole nation is being played out. Remember. Do not forget!"

The columns of people were moving on and on, sometimes at a half run, marching, trotting, without end. There one, there another, would fall and the rest would walk right over them, constantly being urged on by the policemen, "Faster! Faster!" with their whips and rifle butts.

I stood there by the window and watched until about midday when the horror of the march ended.

Now the street was quiet, nothing moved. Corpses were scattered all over, rivulets of blood still oozing from the lifeless bodies. They were mostly old people, pregnant women, children, handicapped — all those who couldn't keep up with the inhuman tempo of the march.

Within a few hours the streets were cleaned up by the men from the small ghetto under the direction of the German and Latvian masters. Stories filtered back. There were over 700 corpses. They were buried in a common grave in the Old Jewish Cemetery, next to the ghetto. There were no tears, no prayers. The bodies were just dumped into a big trench. We were not allowed to go there. The next day an open car with SS officers rode through the streets. The puddles of blood were still there, frozen by now. Not a soul showed himself on the street. The car left, the officers apparently satisfied with the results.

* * *

"Where did they take them?"

"They just couldn't wipe out so many people all at once?"

"I heard they took them to a camp near Salaspils."

"It is hard to believe, after what we saw done here, that they took them anywhere but to the grave."

"I think what they did here was just weed out the old, sick and infirm."

"Yes, why should they destroy manpower that can work, produce for the Wehrmacht without pay and not much food."

"I think they'll send us to some camp and put us to work, maybe dangerous work, like loading bombs, but nevertheless work. The strong will stay alive."

"The main thing is just keeping up with the pace of the march; don't falter, stumble, or fall down."

Speculation continued, rumors, opinions, logical analyses — no facts. We wanted so much to believe that we'd be sent to a camp. We, the ones left in the ghetto, were still too naïve. We could not, or did not want, to believe that our fate would be other than a harsh life somewhere in a camp. The main thing is just to avoid being weak or sick. Just make it through the march. Everybody started training in walking and running around in the house to get ready for the march when the time came.

For several days the ghetto was quiet — like a ghost town. Nobody ventured out. There were no Germans and all the policemen had disappeared. Not a shot could be heard. Gradually some people started appearing on the streets. People started to get together and talk. The general opinion was that nothing like what we had seen would be repeated, that they would let us live out our harsh life in the ghetto. Little by little we were recovering from the shock of what we had lived through and returned to the routine life of the ghetto. The most pressing problem was food. It had to be rationed reasonably to stretch out through the winter.

Our household, too, returned to normal. We cleaned and put things away in their proper places. However, we decided not to unpack what had been prepared for the move, for we might need it.

The ghetto store was opened again. Some differences were noted. Before the Exodus one could obtain products only by presenting a food card; now no card was required. Also, there was plenty of cabbage, potatoes, beets, and carrots. True, they were of poor quality, but this did not matter much in our state. We were so very hungry for vegetables. There was little left at day's end.

Gradually some men from the "Little Ghetto" worked their way back, illegal though it was, through loopholes in the fence, to their families in our ghetto. They told of the sorrow, grief, and anguish of the men who had lost their families, and had no more reason to move back . . .

On the third day of December, rumors started circulating through the ghetto that women dressmakers and seamstresses were required in the city. These would be left in the ghetto and not sent to the camp.

It is common for people to look for any way to save themselves. Many women who could barely darn a sock declared themselves seamstresses. Some women came running to me for instructions on how to run a sewing machine and make a stitch by hand. The same day, a registration of dressmakers and seamstresses began on Maza Kalnin Street, A long line of about 300 to 400 women were there when I arrived. After the registration we were told to go back home to the ghetto, take along food for two days, and come back to the same place at four o'clock in the afternoon. From there we would be taken to the city.

When we gathered that evening with our food parcels, the policemen were already waiting for us. They formed us in columns five abreast and we were on our way. Marching through the "Aryan" streets of Riga, I noticed unusual behavior of the passers-by on the sidewalks. Some followed our column with their eyes full of sorrow, some wiped their eyes, some crossed themselves, they knew more than we did . . .

We crossed almost the entire city. We were brought to the Termincietmus (the main prison) by the railroad station of Brasa. After holding us for some time in the prison yard, we were led to the attic. It was already full of women, seamstresses who had been brought here some days earlier.

As time went on the big door would clank open and more people were pushed in. It got so crowded that people could sit only interchangeably with the ones standing up. The bedbugs and lice had a banquet. The air was foul. Some women had fainted; there was no water and they were revived with difficulty.

We remained in these conditions in the prison for a night and a day. None of the policemen showed themselves. The stink of the air was hardly bearable because of the lack of sanitary facilities. Yet we were still alive. We shared our food with each other. We were plagued by thirst. There was not a drop of water. It looked like we had been brought here to torment us and wear us down.

On the second day the door suddenly opened and the guard shouted: "There is room for fifty people downstairs. Volunteers step forward."

I volunteered. It couldn't be worse downstairs than here in the attic.

The guard counted 50 women and marched us down. It was just as crowded there, too. Besides, the floor was cold and damp cement. There was one little window up in a corner, closed and protected with steel bars.

A woman came by and whispered: "Be careful what you say. That girl over there by the door is suspicious. The Germans probably sent her in as an agent-provocateur."

The cell was guarded here not by a policeman but by a prison guard. There was no food or water here either. A long table stood in the middle. Part of our group slept on it at night huddled together, three or four in a row. The floor was too cold to sleep on.

The next morning the prison supervisor came in. He ordered us to give him a "report." We did not understand what kind of a report and started asking for clarification. This infuriated him. He started shouting at the top of his voice, calling us unprintable names. He finished his tirade by saying that we were undisciplined Jewesses, that shooting was too good for us, and slammed the door behind him.

Another day passed. The atmosphere, physical and mental, was unbearable. Our spirits were broken; we were living dead. How much longer, oh how much longer can this go on? Every passing hour was an eternity. Another half day passed. Suddenly the lock clanked and screeched, the door opened, and there was the supervisor again.

"Everybody must leave the cell immediately."

One woman shouted: "They are taking us to be shot!"

This must have been on many minds. The women

started screaming and did not move. More policemen and prison guards came and started to eject us forcibly. There was great panic.

I did not see that any good could come from resisting. I'd rather be shot anyway than spend any more time in this prison.

"Listen to me," I shouted above the screams. "Listen to me! They are not going to shoot us. They could have done that anytime. Besides, who wants to stay and rot here anyway?"

I walked through the guards and the others followed, apparently calmed down. Out in the prison yard we formed a column and were led into a large corridor of an administration building.

At the end of the long line, near the windows, sat Germans in military uniform. They were sorting the women, some to the right and others to the left. In the group to the right were women whom the Germans designated as seamstresses; the ones to the left were to be sent back to the ghetto.

When my turn came I showed the German officer my diplomas of seamstress, cutter, dressmaker, and fashion designer. He didn't even glance at my papers and motioned me to the left. I tried to protest that I had many years of experience. He didn't even look at me but occupied himself with the next woman.

I thought this was obviously a game, a stall, a deceit. They were dividing us into little manageable groups for easy destruction. The idea crystallized in my mind more clearly every day. There were thoughts to the contrary — why would they destroy useful slaves that demand so little? But this idea grew weaker day by day.

Here I was marching with the "left" column, back to the ghetto. It was so good to be outside, to fill my lungs with fresh air, to talk, oh how enjoyable it was to be walking again. It was the 5th of December.

The ghetto was very quiet. Few people could be seen on the streets. The shutters on all the houses were closed.

Sonia was overjoyed to see me. We spent hours telling each other the happenings of the past few days.

Two more days passed in peace and quiet. Some more men had moved back from the small ghetto. They occupied themselves bringing in water from the outside pump, chopping wood, and occasionally stopping to talk to a neighbor.

6. The Second "Aktion"

Tuesday, the 7th of December, at about 4 P.M. an order was issued and the news spread like wildfire through the ghetto:

"The rest of the ghetto population will be moved this evening. The able-bodied men will go back immediately to the Kasernierungslager. Everybody else should be ready to move, with their packs, at a moment's notice."

Again we were enveloped in fear and panic. For a second time the people were parting in tears, the crying heartrending. The men were telling us to stay together with our loved ones, to help each other, to take few possessions, and for God's sake, keep up with ths pace of the march.

The same scenario as during the first "Aktion" was being played again. Shootings started and were getting more frequent and louder all over the ghetto. This was to scare and paralyze the victims.

At six o'clock it was dark, We heard the shouts of the policemen in the streets: "Everybody out! Everybody out!"

We picked up our packages and knapsacks and ran out into the street.

The Latvian policemen were shouting madly and pushing us to form a column of five in a row. I knew what was coming, with one difference — this time I was a participant, not a spectator. I grabbed the hand of Sonia Bobrov's little girl and Sonia on the other side held the hand of her old mother.

We stood like this for about an hour. Luckily the frost had let up some so it was not too cold. One of the policemen came by and said that mothers with infants and little children and old people would ride in sleighs and that they were to form a separate column. My friend Sonia, her little girl, and her mother decided to ride. We parted with heavy hearts. I told them again and again to keep together, not to lose sight of each other.

After this division was completed, they started driving us, the bigger column, mercilessly, like cattle, cracking their whips and occasionally shooting their guns. When passing along Ludzas Street we were ordered to turn on Liksnas Street and then we were driven into a big three-story building. The building was already full of people, but they pushed us in nevertheless. I wound up on the stairs with my row. There was standing room only. Thus, we stood up all night in fear of falling asleep. One could get trampled to death if he fell on the floor.

On the morning of the 8th of December the shouts of the policemen outside the building began: "Everybody out! Everybody out!"

The human mass shuddered and came into motion instantly. We started pouring out of the building.

At the door stood two Latvian policemen. They were ordering us to hand over jewelry and money. This must have been an illegal operation done in secret from their German SS bosses. Most people were wise to it and just pushed on past them.

Out on the street again, it was good to stretch the dormant muscles and breathe the fresh morning air. It was still dark. On the corner of Liksnas and Ludzas Streets stood a German SS man with a wooden club. He ordered again and again that everyone was to drop his packages on the sidewalk. There were already several truckloads. Mine went, too — all the planning, the packing and repacking that had gone into it — all for some German and Latvian bellies. Deceit. Again and again this thought went through my mind. Our fate was sealed, predetermined — we were going to be destroyed, sacrificed on the altar of Greater Germany. The logic of the past happenings told me this, yet I did not want to believe it.

A young woman was asking the German to let her keep just one little package, a little food for her child.

"Where you are going, everybody is going to eat from one big kettle. There is going to be plenty of food, plenty of food for everybody."

He tore the package from her hands and pushed her with his club.

They were driving us now to the Old Jewish Cemetery. The endless column was guarded on both sides by a chain of policemen armed with automatics. They were shouting commands, demanding that we march in an orderly manner and to watch the rows.

"Atrak! Atrak!" (Faster! Faster!)

The crack of the whips followed the commands. It was dark and very slippery. The snow had melted during the day and now it was frozen and icy. Many people were slipping but were immediately pulled up by their neighbors. Everybody was afraid that the policemen were going to start shooting. Just the same, many people were left on the road trampled to death because of the slippery conditions, the darkness and the fast pace.

Especially bloody was the march downhill of Liksnas Street near the cemetery where we turned on to the narrow Zhidu alley to get on the Moscow Boulevard. On the straight and broad Moscow

Boulevard they drove us almost at a run. It started getting light. Streetcars and pedestrians started appearing.

"How far is it to where we are going?" I asked the policeman near me.

"About seven more kilometers," he strained the words through his teeth.

After the rubber factory "Quadrat," the column turned to the left in the direction of the railroad station Shkirotava. Later we turned to the right toward the railroad station Rumbuli.

At these turns one could see how long the column was. I could not see the beginning or the end of it on either side. The front disappeared into the forest near the Rumbuli Station while the end was still on the Moscow Boulevard — an endless stream of people.

As we came near the forest, we heard shooting again. This was the horrible portent of our future. If I had any doubts left about the intentions of our tormentors, they were all gone now. All I could see before my eyes was a mad dog snarling at me with curled lips, showing vicious fangs. How dear life becomes regardless how hard it is to live.

The situation was hopeless. We were guarded on both sides by policemen and SS men. The little forest was in turn also surrounded by a ring of SS men. Nobody had a doubt as to what awaited us. We were all numb with terror and followed orders mechanically. We were incapable of thinking and were submitting to everything like a docile herd of cattle.

Our column started pouring into the forest. At the entrance stood a large wooden box. An SS man armed with a club stood next to it and shouted over

Naked Riga women before execution (Glavnoye Arkhivnoye Upravleniye, Moscow)

and over: "Drop all your valuables and money in this box."

Surprisingly, most people obeyed the order even though there was no search, and we stopped only momentarily at the box. Rings, bracelets, watches, earrings, bundles of money, were flying over the rim of the box. Whatever did not reach the mark and fell outside the box was pocketed by the fat German.

We were driven on. A bit further a Latvian policeman ordered: "Take off your coat and throw it on top of the rest." There was already a mountain of overcoats.

My brain was working feverishly. The instinct for survival took hold of me. No matter how small, how precarious the chance, I was prepared to take it.

I left my row and ran up to the policeman.

"Look, I am a specialist dressmaker." I showed him my documents and the various diplomas. "I can bring lots of benefits to people. Look at my papers."

"Go show your diplomas to Stalin!" the policeman shouted, and hit my hand with his fist. My papers flew in all directions — my treasured documents — the passport, diplomas, *Ausweise*.

I removed my overcoat and threw it on top of the rest. The policemen were driving still harder. The shooting, the uninterrupted shooting, was becoming louder. We were nearing the end. An indescribable fear took hold of me, a fear that bordered on loss of mind. I started screaming hysterically, tearing my hair, to drown out the sound of the shooting.

"Atrak! Atrak!"

"Take off your clothes! Take off your clothes! Just leave on the underclothes."

Another mountain of clothes. I had on a white

nightshirt on top of a dress and three layers of underwear.

I fell down on the heap of clothes and tried to hide in it. Right away I felt the sharp pain of the whip on my back.

"Get up immediately and take your clothes off."

"I am already undressed," I answered, crying. "I have only a nightshirt on."

"Then go, and no games!"

I went. Still screaming and tearing my hair.

A policeman stopped me and shouted obscenities — why was I not undressed yet? In the same moment another woman ran to the policeman: "My husband is Latvian, see up there, that policeman knows my husband well. I should not die with all the rest of them."

Using this moment, while the attention of the policeman was distracted by the woman, I threw myself on the ground with my face in the snow and lay there feigning death. People were passing me, some stepped on me — I didn't move. A little later I heard voices over me in Latvian: "Look, there is somebody here on the ground."

"Must be dead," a loud voice answered.

Now, I thought, they'll drag me to the trench and that will be that . . . I lay there still as a rock. Then I heard the voices of the policemen: "Atrak! Atrak!"

They were driving the Jews faster, faster. And they ran, and ran, I could hear the tramp of their feet. Right into the grave . . .

I was not fully conscious. A woman, passing by me was lamenting, "Ai, ai, ai . . ." Some object hit me on the back, then another. More objects were falling on me. Finally I realized that these were shoes, because they fell in pairs. I was being covered with shoes, galoshes, felt boots. The load was heavy but I did not dare move a muscle.

I could still hear what was going on around me: "Sh'ma Israel!", an old man cries. Tramp, tramp, tramp.

"Animals! Let the children at least have their clothes in such cold weather."

Crack of the whip.

"Ich sterbe für Deutschland!" (I die for Germany.) Must be a German refugee.

"Death is better than life under these brutes."

"Let me wait until my relatives come so we can die together."

Tramp, tramp, tramp.

More and more shoes were falling on me. I could hear people crying bitterly, parting with each other — and run, run, run. The staccato of the machine guns, the shouts, Atrak! Atrak! The tramp of people's feet running, the cries went on for many hours. Finally the cries and moaning ceased, the shooting stopped. I could hear shovels working not far away. Probably to cover the bodies. I heard Russian spoken. They were being exhorted to work faster. Must be Russian war prisoners. They'll probably be shot, too, after their performance — no witnesses.

A mountain of footwear was pressing down on me. My body was numb from cold and immobility. However, I was fully conscious now. The snow under me had melted from the heat of my body. I was lying in a puddle of water — cold water.

Suddenly I heard Latvian being spoken very close by: "Let's have a smoke."

"A fine performance."

"It was very efficiently organized."

"They have experience."

"Just leave it to the Germans; they are good at it."

"I hope we get our cut of the booty." Pause — "The German have first choice."

"There is enough for everybody."

"I am tired. I am going home."

"Me too."

"Goodbye."

"Goodbye."

After a pause I heard German spoken: "Was suchst du dort?" (What are you looking there for?)

"Ein Paar Strümpfe für meine Frau." (A pair of stockings for my wife.)

Quiet for a while. Then, from the direction of the trench a child's cry: "Mama! Mama! Mamaaa!"

A few shots. Quiet. Killed. Then in German this smug assertion: "From our kettle nobody escapes alive."

I heard footsteps, waited some more. Quiet for a long time. Must be night already. It may be time to leave my hiding place. I was scared to move.

I don't know how long I lay there thinking. My mind was putting things in order. I was still alive! God has chosen me to be His witness. This thought had come to me over and over again. It sustained me through the whole ordeal. I was not a religious woman; I never thought much about it deeply. When holidays came like Rosh Hashana, Yom Kippur, Passover, I went to the synagogue, I prayed; I had no philosophy to my religious feelings. Things were just so — tradition — I never questioned.

Lying there in the cold puddle, things took on a different meaning. Things were not what they seemed to be. There was something miraculous about all that had happened to me. Even after the hours in the freezing puddle of water, I did not feel too badly. There was an inner warmth. Yes, I must live. I must live so that I can tell what has happened to our people. I must fight for my life and God will help me.

I started pushing the heap of shoes away slowly to keep from making any noise. I was out. It was very dark. For a while I remained motionless, listening intently to every sound. There was no wind; it was quiet. I crawled like an animal to where I thought the discarded clothes were and found them. Footsteps! I buried myself quickly under the clothes and waited. Quiet again. There were three heavy blouses one inside the other. They fit. My hand was in a pocket of what seemed like a man's trousers. Something metallic — must be some jewelry — no good. In the other pocker — three cubes, must be sugar — that will be good. Then two woolen scarves. One I wrapped around my neck, the other for my hands. No gloves. They must have thrown them together with the overcoats. On top of everything I pulled over my white nightshirt. This for camouflage — it would blend in well with the white snow. There I was, scared, but dry and warm.

I started crawling deeper into the forest, like an animal on the prowl. Taking a few steps, stopping, listening, continuing on. At one time I heard footsteps and hid behind some trees. But the sound of the steps grew fainter and was gone. I waited. There were some far-off shots. Quiet again.

Here I crawled out of the forest. Now where? What direction? It could be that the Germans were guarding the forest. Will I be able to break out? . . .

7. Wanderings – the Berzinsh Family

I was out in the open and free! The forest was behind me and flatlands before me. Lights were twinkling far away. Must be the railroad station of Shkirotava. Better to stay away from the station. It was hard to make out farmhouses in the darkness. Dogs were barking in the distance — it meant farmers lived nearby. I walked, in a crouch, in the direction I thought I saw silhouettes of houses. I came near a small house, no light was showing, no dog was barking — good.

In the yard stood a booth. I went in — it was an outhouse. I could see the outside through the cracks in the boards. Water started dripping from my clothes. The snow and ice that clung to my clothes during the day was melting. I sat on the seat and leaned back. For the first time in what seemed like an eternity I felt relaxed and comfortable, never mind the smell. Tired, exhausted, hungry, but alive. ALIVE!

. . . I was looking through the keyhole and saw Stalin in military uniform sitting at a desk. He started growing larger and larger like in a movie, then smaller and smaller, then he toppled to the floor with a crash. I woke up and started looking through the cracks.

Two women were coming out of the house. The slam of the door must have wakened me. One of the women carried a lantern, the other a bucket. They went into the stall, must be to milk the cows. It seemed that they were old but I couldn't be sure, it was too dark. After some time they came back. Now I could see that they were old women. I left the outhouse quickly, ran to them and fell on my knees in front of them. I cried and begged them, "Let me stay overnight, please, even if it is in the stall with the cows."

The old ladies were scared stiff. The suddenness of my appearance, my wild looks and actions were indeed frightening. They guessed who I was. The Germans were searching for Jews, Communists, deserters, spies, everywhere and often. The old women stood there motionless.

"For God's sake, only for one night, I beg of you. In the pigsty. Don't turn me away."

They finally regained their composure and said, "Only for one night. You can bury yourself in the hay. We won't give you away. You must have gone through a lot, and we would like to help you, but you know they shoot people for doing this. One night."

I buried myself in the hay. The nightmare of the last couple of days was dissolved in deep sleep.

I was awakened by the two old ladies. It was morning. They brought bread and milk. I ate ravenously, careful not to waste a crumb. Both of them stood there watching me eat with smiles of satisfaction wreathing their faces.

"I don't know how I can thank you, you saved my life. I could not have gone another step."

"We are glad we could help you, my dear. You must have gone through a lot. But now you must leave us; we are afraid for our own lives." The older of the two spoke and the other nodded her head in agreement.

"Couldn't you let me stay one more night?" I begged. "Just one more night? I can work for you. I am strong. I can split wood, milk the cows. I am also a master dressmaker, I can make you new dresses out of old material. What do you say? I must rest up before I can go any farther."

"We will talk it over between us. In the meantime, stay under cover."

"Thank you, thank you, you are so good to me."

They left. I was still alive. There are some good people left in this cruel world. God is leading me. I went back to sleep, the sweet all-healing sleep.

About four or five o'clock in the afternoon I was wakened. The old ladies were very agitated and perturbed.

"You cannot stay here any longer. You must leave. There are searches going on all over the area. Here, we brought you some sandwiches so you won't starve."

"I understand," I said. "You have been very kind to me, and God will be good to you. Where do you think I should go?"

"There," she was pointing with her finger, "there, behind this hillock you'll see a farmhouse. Maybe they'll let you stay there. We are sorry. You are such a nice girl; we are very sorry."

There was nothing to do but to thank them and leave with the sandwiches wrapped in newspaper. It was starting to get dark. I followed a dirt path up the hill. There, leaning on a tree, I saw a youngster about 15 years old. He was well dressed in an overcoat with a fur collar. As he noticed me, he left the tree and started talking in Latvian to me, "Dear auntie, can you help me? They shot all our people. I am the only one who escaped. I have no food and no place to stay. Please help me."

He took me for a Latvian. My heart was wringing

with pain. Poor boy. We both had the same problem. But together it would be even harder for us to save ourselves. I answered him in Latvian:

"I'm sorry I cannot help you. Here, take these sandwiches. This is all I have."

I gave him the sandwiches and left him there without looking back. I felt tears on my cheeks. It hurt inside. A while later I looked back. A huddled little figure under a tree, eating hungrily.

The evening turned to night. It was not cold. I cleared the hill and there were lights blinking at me in the distance, just like the old ladies had said. In a short time I was standing before a small but substantial log house. After a knock on the door, a tall young man opened it. A feeling of warm air glided over my cheeks and there was the good odor of village cooking. Children were playing on the floor; several grownups sat on benches. Everybody's eyes were trained on me with fear. There was a moment of silence, I was thinking of what to say. A young woman got up, ran to the door, and shouted angrily: "Out!"

I was taken aback. The door slammed forcefully in front of me.

It was dark already. The thin path I was following was hard to make out. I was now roaming over fields, marshes, half-frozen mud, falling in snow-covered ditches full of ice-cold water. Every step became a torture; my strength was gone. Then I saw a light in the distance and turned toward it. Another farm. Another house. I knocked on the door.

"Please help me . . ." was all I could say.

"Go while the going is good." I was interrupted. "You are lucky you didn't go to the neighbor's house. There they would have detained you and sent you away where you belong."

More wandering. I lost direction and purpose. My feet were giving out but still dragging me on. Then I stumbled over something and fell with a thump. It turned out to be the wooden front porch of a house. A light was lit in the house and a man opened the door, an old woman behind him. When she saw me she fainted. The man straightened up the woman on the floor and ran into another room for Valerian drops to revive her. In the meantime I had crawled on all fours into the house like a dog, and hid in a crouch under a woodworking bench in the corner. The man came back and revived his mother.

"What are you doing, going around in the middle of the night scaring people to death?"

"Can't you see? I am fighting for my life. I am exhausted, let me stay the night right here."

"Please leave, you cannot stay here, you are endangering all our lives."

"Please, just one night. Nobody will see me. God will repay you for your good deed."

I could see the lines in the man's face soften. There was hope.

"All right, you can stay until tomorrow, but I am afraid to keep you in the house. Go in the back yard and crawl into the stack of hay. If they find you up there, then I am not responsible."

I found a tall haystack in the yard, covered by a roof which was supported by four thin poles. Even today I wonder where the strength came from for me to climb up the slippery pole to the top of the haystack. I buried myself in the hay.

How nice it would be to fall asleep and never wake up, I thought. The cherished sleep was long in coming. Instead, the scenes of the killings rolled before my eyes like a film. I could hear the cries, the screams of the children, the moans, the people running, running . . .

Around me there was absolute silence, not a sound. I heard myself breathing — that meant I was still alive. Was I losing my mind?

In the morning the loud barking of a dog awakened me. A man's voice, "Climb down and leave!"

I didn't answer. I acted as if I weren't there. The dog was barking louder and the man's voice rose with anger: "Come down or I'll make it bad for you."

I climbed down.

"Go, and don't linger around, not for one minute."

There was threat and fear in his voice.

"Thank you for what you have done. I understand. I'll go."

I went wandering on, refreshed by the rest. My mind was clearer. I could think and reason now, make plans. Maybe I should go to Riga. I have so many good Lavian friends there. Somebody will help me. It just cannot be that all of them would throw me out like the farm folks here. They know me up there, I could blend in easily, with so many people in a large city. Here on the farms each stranger is noticed right away.

The air was crisp and clear, the sun was shining for a change. The snow blanketed the fields, its whiteness blinding to the eyes. Here and there footprints of animals and birds could be seen as I plodded along the narrow road made by horses, sleighs, and people. Two dark specks were approaching. Gradually I made out a farmer and a youngster dressed in yellow unfinished sheepskins with rabbit fur hats over their ears.

"How does one get to Riga?" I asked them when they came up.

They stopped. The farmer looked me over, up and down. His face expressed fear and wonder. He couldn't take his eyes off my wretched appearance — without a coat in winter time, with flowery blouses and wrapped head and hands in shawls. Good that I had discarded the white nightshirt.

"Don't be afraid, I will not give you away," he finally said. "You had better not go to Riga. They are checking documents about every corner. You won't have a chance."

He saluted in military style and went on.

It looked as though I couldn't escape. But I wanted to live! Maybe these were my last hours, my last steps alive on earth. I must not die. I have to be a witness. There has to be one witness left. Show me, show me a way to life, oh God! I will tell, I promise I will tell all that I see and hear, so that they shall not forget, we dare not forget.

I was desperate, talking to myself, praying.

I breathed deeply the fresh, cold air. Breathing is life. I will fight for my life. Even if they cut me up in little pieces, each part will clamor for life independently. I will fight to my last breath — I am Thy witness — I swear to You! There will always be time to go to the pits.

I was passing a large white house. It looked prosperous. No sense in stopping there. It would be dangerous. Poorer people have more understanding and by nature have more goodness and compassion. I went on.

After an hour or so I came by a small, dark house. I came nearer and looked through the window. Yes, there were people inside. A knock brought an old farmer to the door.

"Please let me in for a while to warm up," I begged.

"Sure, sure, come in," he said, closing the door behind me. "Come sit by the stove; I just lit the fire."

He brought over a bench. "Here, sit on the bench; the earthen floor is cold and damp. Where are you going?"

I broke down and cried for a long time. It seemed an eternity since I had heard a compassionate voice. I told him between sobs all that had happened to me. He listened with great sympathy and was horrified at the details of the mass execution.

"Poor, poor child," he kept on muttering, "those beasts, those animals, murderers."

"You must be hungry," he said when I fell silent. "I'll fix you something right away."

He brought smoked pork, bread and cheese. I ate and ate until my benefactor stopped me: "You must not eat so much all at once, it will make you sick. Come, I'll make you a place to rest up and you will be hidden from strangers at the same time."

He led me behind some stacks of lumber he was curing in the house for a new building.

"I will go and bring my son and his wife and we'll see where we go from here," he said.

I was asleep in no time.

"Miss, miss, wake up," a young farmer was gently nudging me. "It is dangerous for you to sleep here in the house. We have a safer place for you. My name is Berzinsh."

This was the old farmer's son; his wife stood nearby. They had been told about me. I threw myself at the young woman and kissed her with tears in my eyes. We all cried. I could see they were people with good hearts.

We ate again. They showed me a place in a hayloft for spending the night.

"It is safer here. Crawl into the hay and you'll be safe and warm. We never know when there is going to be a search. And yes, miss, don't be alarmed if one or more men join you during the night. They won't bother you. They will be Russian soldiers hiding out but they will be wearing civilian clothes."

That night a man got up in the loft noiselessly. He, too, buried himself in the hay in another corner. He did not see me.

I stayed in the loft for a full week. The Berzinshes visited me every morning and brought enough food and water for a whole day. They also introduced me to their old mother and the in-laws.

Things were just too good; they couldn't last. A new decree reached my friends. It stated that every house- and landowner was responsible for every person under his roof or on his land. The penalty for hiding people illegally without documents and registration was death.

I had to leave these wonderful, wonderful people. The Berzinshes outfitted me with an old overcoat, woolen mittens, a large woolen (home woven) blanket with fringes on all four sides. They also gave me food. The blanket was of great use and importance to me. First, it was unusually warm; one could wrap it over oneself and be protected from the severest snow storm. Also it was a traditional piece of winter clothing that every farmer's wife used. One could cover head and face, so only the eyes showed. With these three features of the blanket I could stay warm and pass for a peasant woman.

I took leave. The Berzinshes had guilt feelings. I assured them that I understood the situation and that their actions were unique in this part of the world. They had saved my life, at least for now.

"Come back to us when times change," they shouted as I closed the outer gate.

Once again, I was cast out with no place to go. I turned toward a forest, the wind in there was not so strong. The snow was deep and it was hard to walk. On top of this, it began to get dark. I decided to climb a tree and spend the night. Two thick branches forming a wide Y suited me well. I assumed a fetal position, wrapped myself well, and started feeling drowsy with the gentle sway of the tree. It was a very cold night. If I should fall asleep, I might never wake up — this would be a good solution for everything. I fought sleep as long as I could, but nature took its course and I sank into slumber.

I woke with a start. The cold had penetrated through and through. I had lost feeling in my hands and feet. Quickly I managed to get down to the ground and start moving around to get the blood flowing. My extremities started to throb with pain. Thank God they were not frozen. I started munching on some pork fat and smeared some grease on my face and hands. That felt good; pretty soon things returned to normal.

It began to get light. Two women were coming into the forest leading a small sleigh. As they came near, it turned out that this was the old mother Berzinsh and her daughter-in-law. They had come to collect wood.

After listening to how I spent the night and almost froze to death, they decided to help me further.

"You will stay with us for a while as our guest," said the old Mrs. Berzinsh. "We live in a house on the other side of this forest. There is only one house on the farm so you can't miss it. We live on the second floor. Some other people live on the first. Come after dark. Here, have some tea, it is still warm."

The old lady poured some tea from a thermos bottle. It was still hot and warmed my insides.

I helped them gather some fallen tree branches for firewood.

"We'll be expecting you tonight, but do be careful. There are many eyes and ears all around us."

They were off, waving goodbye.

I went to the edge of the forest in the indicated direction to familiarize myself with the area, to avoid unnecessary wandering at night. It worried me that I was leaving footsteps in the snow where one could easily follow me. The forest ended abruptly and before me lay a flat field covered with snow, interrupted here and there by dry stubble. A dark line to my left dissected the field. My eyes followed that line from the forest to a house far away on a hill. This must be a fence or a road. I did not dare venture out of the forest in the daytime, so I stayed just inside and made my way toward the dark line. It turned out that it was a fence, and a road alongside it. This must be the road leading to the Berzinsh house.

At nightfall, I knocked on the door of the house. The old Berzinsh people were waiting for me.

As soon as I came into their house, I felt warmed by the stove as well as by the friendship that one human being radiates to another. These people were taking me into their home at the risk of their own lives; me, a total stranger! When I told them about the little boy I had met and left by the forest, they were very sad.

"If he had come to us we could have saved him. It would have been easier than explain about you to the authorities. We would have sent him to our friends, and they would have kept him as their son. He is not old enough to need documents yet."

It hurt me. It is a shame that I had not decided at that time to take him with me. I could not have foreseen that I would meet some good people. It hurts me to think about that little boy even today.

A few days later we had a visitor: the neighbor from downstairs came up. Mrs. Berzinsh introduced me right away. "Mrs. Zvirbulis, how nice of you to drop in. This is Frida, an old friend of ours. She came to stay with us for a while."

"Frida is a master dressmaker," Mrs. Berzinsh added. "She makes the prettiest dresses, and fast, too."

"Can I make something for you?" I asked.

"My little girl needs a uniform for school with a white apron."

Mrs. Zvirbulis lookd at me first with suspicion, but as the conversation progressed, my free, assured manner and my faultless Latvian dissolved all suspicions. We parted like old friends.

I was glad to be busy sewing. It took my mind off my precarious situation. We had fittings with the little girl and neighborly get-togethers for tea during the next few days. I helped Mrs. Berzinsh with all her chores and managed all the work well. It felt so good to be useful and needed, to be treated and respected as a human being.

This, too, was not to last for long. Mrs. Berzinsh came in one day with the sad news: "They killed the little boy you told me about."

"How did it happen? How do you know?"

"For a short time one or another was hiding him out until he wandered in to the Ulrichs. They took him in, fed him, and turned him over to the police . . . you can guess what happened after that."

We both cried bitterly. This was how the old Mr. Berzinsh found us when he walked in. When we told him what had happened, he said: "I am afraid I too have bad news. I heard rumors in the village that a Jewess is wandering around in these parts. That must be you, Frida. They say the Germans will make a house-to-house search for anyone who lives here without a registration. They are also looking for Russian soldiers who are supposedly hiding out in this area."

We sat for a long while, not saying a thing. Then, "If anyone is caught hiding an 'illegal,' he and his whole family will die and the whole village will be leveled," Mr. Berzinsh quoted.

I hardly slept all night, making plans, thinking of a way out, but to no avail. Nothing made sense, every plan led finally to arrest and the pit.

I was up before the Berzinshes. Hearing me washing, they got up too, lit the stove, and made breakfast. I ate heartily — was this to be my last meal? We parted with tears.

It was still dark when I turned back into the forest, my protector, and wandered all day, back and forth, not daring to leave it during daylight. I was already too well-known in these parts. No solution came to me all day. Here it was night again and fiercely cold. As if by instinct, my route took me to the other side of the forest to the unfinished house being built by the young Berzinshes. I knew there was a stack of straw in the yard and buried myself deep in it. The cold kept me in a state of misery all night. I could barely stand it until morning. In desperation, I knocked on the door. There again were the good faces of the young Berzinshes.

"I must confess that I spent the night in your yard, hidden in the stack of straw. I know that I am subjecting you to terrible danger — but I couldn't think of a thing I could do but freeze to death."

"It is all right, Frida, nobody saw you and you are still alive — that's what counts," Mrs. Berzinsh put her arm around my shoulders.

"I think you should go to the city," Mr. Berzinsh said. "There you can lose yourself much more easily than here. Besides, our house is already under suspicion. Some of our 'good neighbors' are saying we are communists."

"That is because my brother volunteered for the Red Army," Mrs. Berzinsh interrupted.

"And my brother," Mr. Berzinsh continues, "was arrested the second week after the Germans came. We don't even know where he is or whether he is still alive. We expect a search by the police any time now."

I took off my watch from my hand, a "Moser" that I had not dropped in the box before the trench, and put it on Mrs. Berzinsh's hand.

"Have this from me in gratitude for what you did for me, and my expression of friendship."

I quickly remade my overcoat that the Berzinshes had given me so that it had a hump in the back which they stuffed with wool. I put it on, wrapped myself in the fringed blanket so that only my eyes showed and, loaded with a small basket of food, left the Berzinshes. Walking hunched over, I looked like an old peasant woman.

The wind increased and it was getting colder by the minute. It was hard to walk the uneven path the Berzinshes had indicated. I found a long stick which I thought would add even more credence to my appearance; besides, it was good to hold on to on the slippery road. A few passersby mumbled greetings; they didn't pay attention to me.

Thus I plodded on for hours until I reached the city outskirts with its clean sidewalks, on Moscow Boulevard. Suddenly a Latvian policeman came into view, carrying a rifle in his hands, on the ready. I was scared but continued on. He paid me no attention. A little further on came another policeman.

They were guarding the empty ghetto.

The ghetto stood still and dead with the gaping black holes of broken windows and open doors. The scene of the march stayed before my eyes, the shouting, the shooting, the running, the tramp of feet. I wanted to shout . . . With great effort I took hold of myself and plodded on, past the policeman, past the ghetto, under the railroad bridge, and then I was in the center of Riga.

Where to now? Maybe to the janitor of my apartment. He got a lot of my furniture — he might give me one night's lodging in fear I might tell that he had hidden me out. This is going to be dirty, but he deserves it for informing on me in the first place for a suitcase of clothes . . . I was tired, nothing else came to mind.

I rang the bell. The janitor opened the door: "Yes?"

He didn't recognize me. I almost pushed my way in past him.

"I am Frida Frid."

The color drained from his face. He looked scared as if he met a ghost.

"I must have a place to stay for tonight, just one night. You have plenty of my things, you owe me that."

I shot it all out fast, in one breath, not giving him a chance to recuperate. I sat down on a chair.

The janitor's wife joined him now. They were both frightened, casting glances at each other as though consulting about what they should do.

"You cannot stay here. You know what it means to all of us. Go, go wherever you like, but leave as alone.

We won't inform on you, we promise."

I sat there, not moving.

"I have no place to go. I beg you, just let me stay one night; if not I will commit suicide right here."

They both jumped as though they had been hit with something. Each of them caught me by a hand, and they threw me out with such force that I fell sprawling on the stair landing.

"Go to the Lamberts," the janitor's wife hissed, throwing my basket after me. "You gave them more and better things." Slam!

It took a while to collect myself. Maybe I should go to the Lamberts. They did get most of my good furniture. As far as I knew, they were honest, God-fearing people.

Mrs. Lambert, too, did not recognize me. My voice gave me away. Fear showed on her face immediately.

"No, Frida dear, you cannot remain here one minute. Germans visit my son and daughter; they could come here anytime now. You must leave, you really must leave."

I left. Where to now? The German officer? Crazy! But I had worked very hard for him, and he had told me that he respected me for it. What could I lose? My life. I went anyway.

The officer lived on the corner of Elizabeth and Umaras Streets. I had to hurry. The six o'clock curfew hour was approaching. I hurried, dropping all precautions; they were sure to catch me after curfew. I entered the front door and hopped on up to the second floor and rang the doorbell. I was out of breath. The orderly answered. I dropped down on my knees in front of him and begged him to hide me out for the ·night.

"Young lady, I am afraid even to talk to you. Several SS men are living here now, and you know what that means. You had better run from here as fast as you can."

The door slammed in my face.

What now? I ran downstairs and took the back route through the yard. Then I saw the door of the basement was open. I ran down and entered. The basement was flooded and the janitor was pumping water out through a hose pushed through the little square window.

I said to him, "I used to live here. My relatives were all shot and I am the only one left. You can have all that you find in Apartment 35B. Let me stay here over night. I cannot go out in the street anymore because of the curfew. Just one night."

"In 35B some German officers live."

"This is true, but all the furniture is mine," I lied. "When they leave you can have everything."

"I cannot do it. The basement is my responsibility. When they catch you there, it's my head."

"I have only one way out — cut my arteries."

"That is your business, but I cannot help you."

I dragged myself out to the Umaras door. I stood there and thought: this is the end. No way out. As soon as I step outside I'll be caught by the patrols. Better cut my arteries myself. I read somewhere that that is an easy death. One doesn't feel pain, just gradually passes out . . .

I started looking for my little knife in my basket that the Berzinshes had given me. The door opened:

"Psst, psst, go quickly to the top floor, the door leads to the attic," the janitor whispered. "I am not responsible for the stairs and the attic, anybody can wander in."

He was gone. I did not wait for another invitation

110

but started as fast as I could on the dimly lit stairs. An angel had come and saved my life, I was thinking. God is surely helping me. Never again will I have thoughts of suicide, never. God wants me to stay alive, to be His witness. Time and again this thought went through my mind during the whole ordeal. I clung to it. It gave me comfort and peace of mind in the most dangerous situations.

I stole past the familiar officer's apartment and up, up as far as the stairs went. The door, no there was no door, just a dark opening staring before me.

Dark inside. In normal times it would have frightened me to enter but now the darkness offered comfort and protection. I felt my way around in the darkness until I touched what seemed to be a large wooden box. It was filled with empty bottles. I sat on it and rested to catch my breath and recover myself.

I listened to what was going on around me. In the apartment below they were having a party — music, laughter, dancing. In the next one over, the same thing plus drunken singing, then someone telling a story and an explosion of laughter.

As soon as I had rested, my mind turned to the sights and sounds of the execution march. The shouts, the moans, the screams, the pleadings of the thousands marching in columns to their doom, the crack of the whips, the shots, the tramping of feet, running, running . . .

Suddenly a door on the lower floor opened and two people came out on the stair landing, then up the stairs right to the attic. I froze — here they'll catch me. One lit a match and started forward in a drunken manner.

"Hey! This is an attic, where are we going?"

"Come on, let's go back."

They left. Safe again. I breathed deeply. I sat there the rest of the night, afraid to sleep. In the morning, after I heard the first steps of people on the stairs, I left my hiding place and wandered all day in the city. With nightfall I returned to the same attic for two more nights. My provisions supplied by the Berzinshes were getting low. It was good that they had also given me 100 marks. I could buy a glass of tea once in a while, choosing the shabbiest places, places I would have been afraid to step foot into before the war. I would have to find another place to sleep. It was dangerous to stay too long in one place. Who could I go to now? Perhaps my old "Aryan" friends?

Mezhulis! It struck me like lightning. They were such nice people — I'll try. With renewed energy I made my way to 32 Shprenga Street and knocked. They let me in — no recognition. I told them who I was and immediately the old friendship returned. I had to tell all that had happened to me. They listened attentively with tears in their eyes. During the Ulmanis dictatorship Mr. Mezhulis was an officer. Now he was a superintendent.

"Frida," he said to me, "on Getrudas Street (now Karl Marx) there is an empty apartment. It has a very simple lock. You can open it with a little knife. You can go and stay there. Don't make any noise and nobody will bother you."

They fed me and then I went to the given address. My little knife was working on the lock but with no success. Then I heard footsteps which sent me running upstairs. After the people had gone I was back working on the lock, again with no luck. So I went back to the Mezhulis' and told them about my ineptness.

"But this is so simple, Frida," Mr. Mezhulis said.

"You put the blade into the lock opening about three centimeters, then lift the blade under about a forty-five degree angle until you touch something and twist slowly. When it clicks, the lock is open. Never mind, I have another apartment that is empty. That door is open, it doesn't even have a lock. You will have to be very quiet there because it is a wooden frame building and only the one other apartment below is occupied."

I ran off elated that now I would have a place to stay.

It was an old, wooden frame, small, two-story building on the corner of Gertrudas and Avotu Streets. I went upstairs quietly and sure enough, the door was open. Jews had lived here before, the *mezuzahs* still hung on the door posts. The house was small and empty, not a trace of life except for a sardine can filled with frozen water. The water faucet was frozen, there was no toilet and the place was dirty. The windows were broken and the cold wind was free to come and go — cold. Just the same, I was glad I had a roof over my head for the night.

An old newspaper from my basket spread on the wooden floor made my bed and general living space. I sat on the floor contemplating my situation, picturing myself alone on a life raft, in a stormy ocean, thrown by the waves, blown by the winds, a darkened sky, no hope for help — no hope. No hope? This is not true, I argued with myself. I had my life raft and the others didn't. I was given a chance — many chances in fact. Someone is looking out for me. I must help Him. I must not give up. I must fight and claw to stay alive. I have a mission, a duty to perform. I must stay alive — I am Thy witness.

I closed my eyes and I saw my relatives, my friends with their dear, smiling faces. Then their smiles changed into fright, anguish, horror, and they screamed and shouted and ran and ran endlessly into the pits and the machine guns pierced them like blown-up balloons and blood spurted . . . I wanted to scream but my throat was choking up and no screams would come, I began falling and falling, down, down, darkness, no bottom, no end . . .

I must have fallen asleep. I woke wet with cold perspiration, my heart pounding, my hands hugging the basket. It was still dark outside. Have I made noises in my sleep? Has anyone heard me? I sat listening intently. The noises from below were the same. Seems that some mechanic lived there who fixed things. I heard a hammer beating on metal, a motor running, filing noises, grinding noises — no change. Good. I stayed awake now, sleep would not come.

I sat there for hours, silently, without motion. The moon was shining on the left-over broken glass. I enjoyed looking at the flowery designs nature had painted on the glass. It gave me hope and solace. I will have to pull myself together, fight for my life — patience. Maybe another few weeks and the Russians will come back. The main thing is to overcome the cold, the terrible miserable cold.

The next day I went outside to walk and get warm. A glass of hot tea felt good. I bought a newspaper and returned to my apartment to pass the time reading. It looked like the Germans were winning all the battles. They were advancing on all fronts. This made me depressed. What if the war protracts into a year or two? How can I hold out?

The cold, the merciless cold! I learned that the newspapers helped keep my feet warm. The next day I bought two newspapers. It was good for reading and for covering up.

The papers said that the Germans were doing well, but something in an editorial told me not really all that well. It merely said that all the reverses the Germans were suffering were caused by the Jews and Bolsheviks. They must be wiped off the face of the earth. There was a spark of hope. They do have troubles. Not everything was as rosy as they would make it out to be. The requisitioning of blankets, felt boots, fur hats for the military was also a good sign — the cold was hurting them.

The freezing temperatures were hurting me, too. The *Tevia* (Fatherland in Latvian) newspapers were serving as extra blankets. Lying still and sleeping requires less food and gives the brain a rest. My food basket was just about empty. Will need to replenish somehow. On that thought I went to sleep.

When I woke up my body felt ossified, paralyzed. There was no feeling in my legs, my throat was dry and sore, my eyes wanted to stay closed — I am frozen, ran through my mind. Frantically I started rubbing my hands, feet, neck. Every part of my body was hurting. Well, if it hurts, then I am still alive, I thought. I kept rubbing and exercising until the blood circulation was restored.

It became clear to me that I couldn't remain there much longer. The cold would accomplish what the Germans tried to do. I decided to go again to the Mezhulises.

They took me in as before. Their hospitality knew no bounds. They fed me and made me drink several glasses of tea laced liberally with honey and raspberry preserves to make me perspire. I finally warmed up.

"I simply cannot understand why you could not open the lock of the other apartment," Mr. Mezhulis was saying. "It is warm there, it has a toilet and running water. Here, let me show you again how to go about it. Give me your little knife. . ."

The doorbell rang. The Mezhulises went to the door while I hid in a closet, an ear to the wall.

"Have you seen or heard from a girl named Frida Frid?" I recognized the loud voice of Miss Krison.

"No, we haven't seen her since long before the war," Mrs. Mezhulis said in an even tone.

"We heard that she escaped and is wandering around," said another female voice that I did not recognize.

"We told you she hasn't been here."

"She was making clothes for you, and we hear you were very friendly. If she comes calling, you be sure to report it. You know what it means to you, don't you?"

The door closed. I left the closet after a while. The Mezhulises stood there, shaken.

"That was your 'friend' Krison with the daughter of the building janitor of your apartment," Mrs. Mezhulis said after a pause.

"Yes, now they'll be watching you. I better leave and I won't come to see you again."

They refilled my basket with dried bread, sausages, dried cheese, a jar of honey, and dried apples. We parted with tears in our eyes.

I decided to try my luck again on the lock of the apartment on Gertrudas Street. I turned and twisted my little knife blade in all directions, pushed, pulled, and twisted the knob without success. You are a real "Shlimazl" I told myself — you will never be a safe-cracker. After a few interruptions caused by people going and coming, I gave up.

What now? Back to the cold, empty room. Another couple of days passed. This was an extraordinarily cold winter and it was getting colder. I was trying to keep in motion all the time, sleeping in short snatches. My throat was sore. I dared not get sick. My strength was waning with each day.

I decided to see the Mezhulises again. The door did not open on my prearranged faint knock. Instead, the Mezhulises' little daughter's voice sounded through the door: "My parents say they cannot let you in anymore. Our house is under suspicion and surveillance."

Back on the street. I tried my voice and could not recognize it. It sounded somewhere between the crow of a rooster and the bark of a dog. I must warm up. After an hour or so I went again to the Mezhulises. This time nobody came to the door.

I went back wandering the streets senselessly, trying to think of something to get me out of my predicament. Large posters were pasted everywhere. I stopped to read one. In large bold print it said:

"Anyone reporting to the authorities a suspicious person or a hidden Jew will receive a large sum of money and many other gratuities and privileges."

I did not stop long enough to read the details of the finer print. This was one way I could get rich, I mused to myself, reporting one Jewess hiding out, half frozen.

I wandered into the Ziedonu Park at the intersection of Maria (now Suvorov) and Artillery Streets. At the entrance stood a public toilet. I went in — paradise, it is warm inside! I ran to the stove, a wonderful, up-to-the-ceiling big brick stove. I put my hands on it — bliss. Then I put my whole body against it and rotated from side to side. I had already started making plans to come here every day. As soon as somebody came in for necessities, I ran to a booth and sat on the stool, not to attract attention. When the people left, I was back hugging my friend the stove. I felt my body thawing out — it was so pleasant. My voice was still hoarse, my hands had blisters full of water.

From time to time the keeper would come in, but she paid no attention to me, same as the other people.

On the next day, I ran to the park early in the morning. The stove was on my mind all night. As I stood there and warmed myself, a young girl in her twenties came in, well dressed, with lots of makeup. She came to the stove too, and started warming herself.

"I am meeting someone here," she said.

"Me, too," I said.

After a while an old lady with a dirty face and unkempt hair came in, in ragged clothes, dirty torn shoes, rotten socks with holes at the heels — a tramp. She was hunched and thin. The two women ran to each other, hugged and kissed.

"How long, how long has it been since I've seen you?" moaned the old lady. "How are you, Lilita, how are things with you?"

"I came to Riga without my husband," Lilita answered. "I am staying with a friend. How are you doing, Auntie, you don't look so well."

"I live like a tramp. I have no papers, no food card; I stay wherever I can find a place, sometimes in an attic, sometimes in a barn. People feed me and give me their old clothes, sometimes even money when I catch them on Sunday after church."

I was puzzled — the old lady did not look Jewish, why did she live like this?

Lilita in the meantime opened her bundle and took

out a sack of hard, dried black bread toast, offered some to the old lady, and to me. too.

"Listen, dearie," Lilita was saying, "I'll give you an address. Go to Skolas Street 10; for one mark you can stay there overnight. The landlady there does not register anybody, which will be just the thing for you. Tell her that Lilita sent you."

"No," replied the old lady, "I won't go there. She'll take one look at me and throw me out. I have a place . . ."

I almost cried out from excitement — how wonderful! I wasn't listening any more. The two women kept on talking for a while longer and left. I remembered the address well — Skolas 10. What if I should go there and say "Lilita sent me." No registration, one mark per day — could one ask for more or better?

A thin, emaciated old lady, about 55 or 60, opened the door. "What do you want?"

"Lilita sent me. I came from a faraway village and haven't been able to locate my relatives in town. I caught a cold on the way and would like to stay here overnight."

"Well, if Lilita sent you, you can stay. Come, follow me."

She led me upstairs. Her apartment was in the attic. It consisted of one room and a kitchen with a skylight. The room was divided by a long folding screen. She showed me a large wooden bed and a deep soft chair nearby.

"This is where you sleep. There by the kitchen is the toilet."

She started coughing as she walked out behind the screen and had a hard time stopping. When she stopped, I ventured on the other side of the screen.

119

The landlady sat on a low tripod stool by the bed. Another old lady was on the bed; she paid no attention to me.

"Can I have a glass of hot tea? My throat hurts badly," I asked.

"I'll give you tea but sugar is in short supply."

"I have my own sugar."

The hot liquid felt good in my throat even though it hurt with every swallow. It warmed me up somewhat. I took off my overcoat and, without taking off my clothes, stretched out on my bed. I fell asleep with the heavenly feeling of being warm and a bed under me.

A man's voice woke me up. The landlady led a man into the kitchen and they talked in a low voice. All I could hear was the landlady saying ". . . she is young and good looking, right off the farm . . ."

Like lightning I jumped out of bed, rolled up like a ball in the chair and covered myself with my overcoat. No sooner had I done that than the silhouette of a man approached the bed. Finding it empty he lit a match and found me cowering in the chair.

"Ah, there you are, my little dove. Don't be afraid of big Anton. Big Anton is gentle with little girls."

A huge hulk of a man stood over me in the darkness reeking of vodka and tobacco. He grabbed me by the shoulders. I screamed, "Get away from me! Dont touch me!"

He reeled back and went to the landlady, complaining, "What is the matter with this girl? Who is she?"

"I don't know. Lilita sent her. She probably has the monthly."

This apparently satisfied him. He mumbled some kind of obscenity under his breath and slammed the door behind him.

"What kind of primadonna do you think you are? I

stalled this guy off, but another may come."

"What goes on here, I don't understand?"

"Lilita sent you here, so what are you asking questions for? Hasn't she told you?"

"I will pay you well to stay over. Only let me have peace tonight."

"No. I have clients, and I need young girls for them. Lilita too comes here, only she brings her own clients."

"I have a very bad cold; I must have rest. I will pay you the same that you receive from a client."

That mollified her.

"All right, I won't let anybody in tonight."

I went back to bed reassured.

Again there was a knock on her door. I heard German conversation through the closed door. Then I heard the door open and the German came in. The landlady told him, between fits of coughing, that tonight she had no girls for him. He was stubborn.

"How about you?"

"Go on, you flatter me, an old one like me." Cough, cough, cough, spit. "I hope you are not afraid of contracting tuberculosis?"

"Maybe you are right. I better come back another night."

He was gone.

"How many more are you going to let in? I thought we had an understanding."

"This one I couldn't refuse. He is one of my best clients. Besides, he brings sausages and salamis and these you cannot buy for gold."

"I need some peace and rest to get over that damn cold."

"You can rest now. I doubt if anyone else is going to come tonight."

It was as she said — a peaceful night. In the morning the landlady started coughing so much that it scared me.

"What is it, can I help you?" I asked.

"This damn tuberculosis eats out my innards. What is it to you? I'll be all right after a while." Then: "Aren't you playing around with men? You could make a lot of money, you know."

"I am not judging you for what you are doing, but I could not live like that even if I were threatened with death, or for mountains of gold."

"Everyone lives his own way. That is his business."

"Could I stay for one more night? I beg you, decline your clients for a few days. I will pay you for everything. I have money."

"All right. I don't mind having a little peace and quiet myself."

I was very pleased at this turn of events. That day the landlady fed me a hot dinner and treated me to smoked sprats. A few more days like this and I would be rid of my cold.

The second evening came. The landlady said it was Christmas. Shots of firecrackers were heard from the streets. Fireworks lit up the sky which we could see only occasionally through the skylight.

At night again, knocks on the door almost continuously. My landlady began to get perturbed. "I don't know how long I can keep them away. They can get mad and report me. What I am doing is illegal, besides it may hurt my business."

I prayed for morning to come. I lay on my bed and tensed with every sound. Finally morning came. I paid off the landlady and before I left I asked, "Do you know of a place where I could go and stay for a few days without being bothered and without registration? I left without papers."

"Yes, I know of a place but that landlady does the same thing I do. On top of that, her walls are made of plywood and you can hear people even whispering in the next apartment. I don't know of any others. You'll have to find a place yourself."

I left. Again back to the empty, cold apartment and the newspapers on the floor. My cold was getting worse. I strained my memory for the names and addresses of my "Aryan" friends. Sifted them through my mind. One name popped up — Sokolov — a Russian family that I had befriended long before the war. They lived somewhere on the Moscow Boulevard but the actual number of the house escaped me; I vaguely remembered the area.

Next day I went looking in the general area for the name on the directories of many houses — no luck. Then all of a sudden it struck me: Spers! The mother and daughter Spers had rented a room in my apartment until 1938. Why didn't I think of them before? I knew where they had moved also.

But they had moved from there too. I decided to risk a visit to the police address bank. There was a long line and I decided to sit a while in a chair and rest. A pleasant warmth emanated from the hot stove and because I was tired from the long walk and the sleepless nights, I fell asleep. I woke with a start. There were few people left by now, and I was afraid to be found out. I put on a bold face and put in my request. I received a card with an address. Hitlerstrasse 101 (now Lenin Street).

I almost ran to the address. Finally, finally, I would see some close friends.

The old Mrs. Spers opened the door. The mother and daughter looked at me thinking some tramp had come for a handout. They did not recognize me because of my clothing and my rooster-like voice.

"Remember Frida? You rented a room at my apartment at Krišjana Barona 15/13. By a miracle I escaped death and now I am wandering from house to house. Have pity on me; please help me. Hide me out for a while. If not I'll perish."

I spoke fast; in one breath I told them everything, not giving them a chance to hesitate or reply.

They were stunned. The old lady was shaking and murmuring, "Jesus, Maria." The daughter stood there with her hands on her face and eyes full of fear. Finally she said, "We have friends who drop in often, one is from the Secret Police . . . we could all be shot."

"I will crawl into some dark corner and nobody will hear or see me. Just for one night," I begged.

They stood there as if glued to the spot, as if they had lost their speech. They did not say Yes or No. I did not wait long for an answer but ran inside the kitchen pantry and closed the door behind me.

They did not chase me out that night, but they didn't let me stay again. I went there several times, rang the bell, knocked on the door — nobody answered.

I was convinced now that none of my city friends would extend a hand to help me. My food and my money, no matter how I rationed myself, were running out. Back to the farm — my last hope — the Berzinshes.

It didn't take me long to pack and move out of "my apartment." Here I was, trudging the streets of Riga again. I was bold now and did not avoid passing policemen. I walked like I belonged, like I had the right, like I had a purpose. Wrapped in my shawl so only the eyes showed, hunched to add about twenty years to my age, I shuffled along and nobody bothered me.

There, I was passing the barbed wire fence of the ghetto — just a glance, a pain in my chest. Out of town now — Rumbuli — my tens of thousands of brothers and sisters, I haven't forgotten you, I am still alive, I am your witness . . .

At twilight I was nearing a farm. I opened the door to a house. A drunken old man, his daughter-in-law, and several small children trained their questioning eyes on me.

"May I stay here overnight?" I asked in Latvian. "I've walked from Riga and it is still too far to make it to my friends' house before nightfall."

"Sure," the old man said. "We are always glad to have company."

"Mainly, I'd like to warm up. I am frozen through. If you don't mind, I'll sit by the stove."

"I'll fix you up so you can stretch out your feet right up to the stove," the young woman said.

She brought a board and fastened it so I could stretch out my legs on it and touch the hot bricks while sitting on a bench. I am warm now, what could be better?

The family was getting ready to eat dinner. I, too, was called to the table. A large pitcher of milk stood in the center of the table. There were bowls of cottage cheese, potatoes fried with pork and onions, and slices of black bread. They watched me to see if I would reach for the pork. I did and even said that it was very tasty. I had passed the "test" and had ingratiated myself with the young woman. She was glad to have someone to talk with. I was hungry and ate my fill. Soup was served to wash down the meal.

"No, thank you," I said, "I am full. I would like to have a glass of tea though if I may. My throat is very sore."

"City folks who live on what they get on the food cards don't eat much," the old man kept the conversation going.

"You can get used to anything when you have to," I put in.

The conversation went on lazily for a while. We washed the dishes and put things away, then to bed. The young woman went with the children into the bedroom. The old man took a few swigs of vodka from a bottle on the shelf, sat down on the bed in the corner, and started undressing. I blew out the kerosene lamp. Now only the flickering light of the stove illuminated the room. I lay down on the floor near the stove and covered myself with my overcoat.

"Hey, hey, come sleep with me," the old man whispered. "My bed is softer than the floor, and it is more fun, too."

"Thank you," I replied. "I am fine here."

He came close to me in his underwear, squatted down, and whispered: "What kind of a girl are you? I am a good man, you'll see. Have no fear of me. You won't get pregnant."

"I can't do it. I have the monthly." (I learned.)

That stopped him for a while. Then, "Just let me kiss you and fondle you a little bit."

"You want to catch my cold? Don't you hear how hoarse I am?"

That did it. He went to his bed grumbling. I stretched out my feet and touched the hot bricks — it was heaven. The heat gradually penetrated my body and I relaxed in a deep sleep. I woke once and it took me a while to remember where I was. The old man was snoring evenly; I went back to sleep.

The young woman was first to get up in the morning. I followed immediately. My throat felt much better and my voice sounded more like my own. Two or three nights like this one would make me well.

The old man got up, too. He didn't seem very friendly toward me; he felt offended. I would have to leave.

"I would like to pay you for the food and putting me up for the night," I said to the young woman.

"Never mind," she replied. "It looks like you could use the money yourself and a good meal, too. You were good company. We don't get too many visitors."

We parted and I was on my way. The old man followed and walked with me in silence. When we were far enough from the house not to be overheard, he shot out, "You fooled me last night, you bitch."

"I saved you from sin."

"Sin, hell, if my son had been here you wouldn't have left like this." He turned back. He had gotten it off his chest.

Some kilometers later I was with the Berzinshes. They were genuinely glad to see me alive. "We often wondered if you made it to the city," the old Mr. Berzinsh said. "We hear that they check documents often."

"She has a guardian angel," his daughter-in-law added.

I told them everything that had happened; they begged for every little detail. As I spoke I could see from their expressions that they felt deeply for me and all that I had been through. Sometimes they showed pain, sometimes compassion, and once in a while there was a smile.

"Oh, my poor dear," the daughter-in-law exclaimed and embraced me. "God is with you, I can see that. He has made you strong to withstand all the dangers."

The whole family got together to decide my future.

"Our house is being watched," young Mr. Berzinsh began. "You cannot trust anybody nowadays. Your best friend or neighbor could inform on you. Everybody is under suspicion and is himself suspecting."

"Frida cannot stay here for her own good," the old man said. "If she is seen only twice by someone, we'll have the police here."

"But where can I go?"

"For the time being, go back to your empty apartment in the city," the old man instructed after a long silence. "It seems that that is your safest place. Right now go to the forest and wait for us there. We'll prepare a basket of food for you that should last you about two weeks. We'll give you some money, too. After that come back here. By then we'll have thought of a plan for you."

I was on my way back to the city with my laden basket. A thick, wet snow started falling and the weather grew warmer. At times the snow was so thick I could not see my way ahead. The trail was now covered with snow and I walked along it mostly by instinct. I found my way back and was once again on the floor of "my apartment." The frost had let up some and I could keep myself reasonably warm.

From sounds that were coming from the side wall, I gathered the apartment next door was being refurbished to be rented. What if they decided to do the same to mine? I had no place else to go, so there was no reason to worry about it, I decided lightheartedly.

So passed day after day in solitude and fear. Two weeks went by — time to head back to the Berzinshes, even though I still had food left and money, too. I knew my way pretty well by now and was experienced in walking long distances. I could walk ten or even twenty kilometers without a rest.

There was the Moscow Boulevard again; I was walking without fear now. From a side street two policemen appeared leading a group of women with knapsacks on their backs.

Rumbuli. They hadn't finished with their horrible deception.

I wanted to shout, "Run for your lives; they are leading you to slaughter! Run! Maybe some of you can save yourselves!" I didn't do any such thing. There was no use, my reason was saying. Tears were choking my throat. I quickened my pace and soon they were far behind me. Now I let the tears pour down my face.

I was out of the city when a chilly wind started, penetrating all my clothing, clear to the bone. I stopped at a farmhouse to warm up.

"I would like to warm up a bit in your house," I told the lady. "I'm walking from the city to some friends on a farm to replenish our food supplies. One cannot make out on the food cards."

"Come sit by the stove," she welcomed me in. "Food must be scarce in the city, judging by the many people who pass by. At least the Germans got rid of all the Jews. Now we can breathe clean air."

I sat by the stove and looked away so she could not see my face. She doesn't recognize me, I thought — good for both of us.

"You must be hungry after such a walk," my bene-factress continued. She cut a slice of black bread and smeared it thick with lard. "Here, this will keep the cold away."

The bread was freshly baked with a crust that crunched with each bite. After a bit of small talk and "pockets full of warm air" I took off again, thanking the lady for her hospitality. A few more kilometers brought me to the Berzinshes.

They were taking me in now like a member of the family. They already lived in the semi-finished house. I was given hot milk to warm me. Again the family council began: what to do with Frida. Various plans were proposed and rejected. Finally old Mr. Berzinsh, scratching his head, said: "Some time ago I knew an old lady by the name of Pesla. She was a little touched in the head, senile and very religious and superstitious, a Seventh Day Adventist. She lived in Chiekurkalns, near Riga. I don't remember her address exactly, but after you cross the railroad track from the main road, turn immediately to the left. The third or fourth house from the corner is Pesla's. It is a little ramshackle house; you cannot miss it. There is only one like it."

"Will she trust me?" I asked.

"I am coming to that. The approach to her must be special. You have to come there on a Friday, close to evening. Saturday is her holy day — Sabbath. We will have to help her with food products."

"Who should I say I am?"

"Now don't laugh. Tell her that you were sent by the angels from heaven to help her. Don't worry, she'll believe you and take you in. When the food runs out come back here and we'll always replenish it."

We decided on this plan and parted with much hugging and kissing. Laden again with a full basket, I left. The familiar road took me through the forest, to

Moscow Boulevard. There again my head turned toward the double barbed wire fence — the ghetto. It was empty, quiet, dead . . .

I spent one more night in "my apartment," for tomorrow was Friday. I was excited, looking forward to a new adventure.

8. Pesla

Chiekurkalns was a small place, right outside Riga. I crossed the railroad tracks, turned left into an alley toward a little house, badly in need of repair and crying for paint. This must be it. I could feel my heart beating faster as I knocked on the door and asked, "Does Pesla live here?"

"Who are you?"

"I was sent by the angels from heaven to help you. Let me in, please."

"I am in bed and it is hard for me to get up," an old voice grumbled.

"My dear, it is already Friday and late. I must give you the presents I brought for you. I cannot wait."

I heard a bolt click and the door opened. A tiny old lady dressed in a nightgown was running back into bed as I entered the house.

"Forgive me, my dear, that I greet you in bed. It is dark and cold. I feel better in bed. Who are you and where do you come from?"

"I came to help you. I have gifts of food."

"I knew you would come. They told me you would come someday when I least expected you. I hope you can stay with me for a while. I am lonely and feeble."

"Yes, yes, I'll stay with you," I was quick to assure her. "I need you more than you need me."

I fell to my knees, embraced the old lady and broke out crying long and hard. Pesla was stroking my hair, saying, "There, there, have a good cry, my child, and God will help us."

It felt so good being caressed, as though she were

my own mother. I needed so much to open up the welled-up feelings, to pour my heart out to someone and have a good cry.

"Tell me, dear, what bothers you. Old Pesla will pray and the Almighty will help us."

I started telling my horrible story, who I was, and what had happened to me. She listened and kept on stroking my head.

"This is a miracle, God's miracle. The children of Israel have perished and you, you alone, God has saved and sent to me. How grateful I am for His trust in me. I am going to guard you like a holy one. You alone have to stand for your whole tribe. I am going to love you and guard you like my own daughter."

I lay with her in bed in a gentle, loving embrace. Gradually I calmed down and fell asleep with a happy feeling in my heart.

I was up with the first light of day.

Pesla's bed stood in a corner of the kitchen. The cooking plate was covered with empty pots which hadn't been washed in ages. A little table and a stool completed the furnishings.

In my state of desperation, I was overflowing with happiness at having found a safe place to stay, and I hadn't been aware of the stench that stood in the air. The house swarmed with cats, all sizes, colors, breeds. They were everywhere and they were not house trained. Their droppings were everywhere. Poor Pesla didn't see any need to clean up.

I started the chore right away. Pesla got up in a very fine mood. She stopped my work to show me into a second room. It was furnished with a buffet, a large table, three Vienna chairs, and an old organ. In the corner by the stove was a heap of wood for burning. Trash and junk abounded everywhere.

Back in the kitchen I took food out of my basket —
cottage cheese, bread, butter, eggs —and cooked our
breakfast. We ate well. It seemed that Pesla hadn't
had a good meal in a long time. She was very happy.

"The Almighty remembered me and sent you to me
to carry out His wish. We must pray and be grateful."

She picked up a thick German bible from the organ
and found the place where it says why God's wrath
had come upon the Israelites. She made me kneel and
she said, "We have to pray to God, sing psalms to
Him, and I'll play the organ like King David did. God
heard his voice and granted him eternal reign."

Pesla was cross with me because my praying was not
too enthusiastic. She sat before the organ and started
playing and singing. She made me sing with her and
repeat after her. Her spirited, joyous singing and
praying did not go well with the suffering in my
heart. I was forcing myself and putting out a half-
hearted effort to please Pesla. She was a simple,
good-hearted, and devoted person.

"Bless the Almighty God day and night. Pray to
Him and He will answer your prayers and help you."
Again and again Pesla repeated this to me.

We spent all day Saturday singing and praying.

Sunday I continued cleaning. I dusted the walls and
furniture, scrubbed and washed the caked-on cat
dung from the floor, fixed a box with sand for the
animals, and started scouring the pots and cooking
stove.

"You need not wash the dishes and pots," Pesla said
trying to stop me. "My dear little kittens lick them
clean and dry. There is nothing cleaner than a cat's
tongue."

I did not share her opinion and kept on with the
scouring. I was appalled when I got to Pesla's bed. It

was a horrible mess. The sackful of straw was permeated with cat and human excrement. The straw was rotten all the way through. She had no linen which was why she slept in her clothes and wrapped up in her overcoat. Luckily she had a few tablecloths from which I fashioned a new sack. In the backyard was a little barn where someone used to keep a horse. I found enough straw there and hay to stuff the new sack for Pesla to sleep on.

Then I started on Pesla. I washed her, even though she protested that she was "born clean." I changed her clothes and washed her old ones.

My Pesla came to life. By evening, everybody and everything was clean. The stench was gone, and we weren't hungry. She was convinced that I had been sent by God to deliver her from hunger and make her happy.

We decided that I would sleep in the big room. It was colder there, but safer, away from the eyes of curious visitors. The air there would be fresher, too.

The order I had brought to the house did not last long. The sand box was ignored by the cats. Pesla, too, had her ways of living in filth. I was fighting a losing battle.

Pesla was very generous with her love and affection. She always wanted to do something pleasant for me. She remembered that last fall she had put up some green tomatoes from her own little garden. She brought out the jar and opened the lid. The tomatoes were covered with a scum of mold. I skimmed off the mold and tasted the salty brine. It tasted good to my hungry stomach — I ate it all. In a little while I started having sharp cramps. Pesla forced me to go to her doctor who lived in Chiekurkalns.

"You have an ulcer," the doctor diagnosed, "but

don't be alarmed, it isn't dangerous. I'll prescribe some good pills, stay in bed for a few days with a hot pad and it will go away."

The doctor started writing the prescription. "Your passport, please?"

I was shaken. After a moment's hesitation, I started looking in my bag. "I don't seem to have my passport with me. I must have left it at home."

"All right. I'll write the prescription and you can fill in the number of the passport yourself, here on top."

The doctor handed me the prescription form, I paid for the visit, and came back home. I did not dare to have the prescription filled. We heated some water, filled three glass bottles and tied them to my stomach with a towel. I lay down on my floor bed, wrapped myself in my overcoat with several books under my head. The pain subsided a little. I began to feel drowsy and lost myself in a deep sleep . . .

Pesla thought I had died many times. Only occasionally did I show signs of life. When I came to, I felt very weak and wanted to keep lying on the hard floor, which felt like soft down.

"You were a very sick girl, Frida," Pesla started telling me when she realized that I was really awake. "You were out like this for twelve days. I barely got some hot tea into you once in a while. You were dead many times, so I prayed and dear God revived you again and again. Now, get up on your knees and pray to Him yourself."

When I sat up, the whole room started turning. I had to hold on to the floor to keep from falling over.

"My little daughter, we are completely out of food. I used up all my coupons as well as the food that you brought for myself and my kittens. Now maybe you can go out and bring some more food to the house."

"I am very weak, I have hardly enough strength to stand up. I should eat something first."

Pesla was thinking out loud: "Some time ago I was standing on a chair and removing a little sack of flour from the top shelf of the buffet. The sack broke and about half of the flour spilled. I thought to clean it up later, but forgot about it."

I wove my way to the buffet. There really was a little mound of flour. The thought of food gave me strength. I brought a pot and knife from the kitchen and scraped off all the flour. After I removed from it all the mouse droppings I could find, I added salt and water and cooked up a kind of gruel. Pesla and I had our fill, and some left over for the cats.

I could feel my strength returning by the minute. The dizziness disappeared.

"Now, let us pray to the Almighty and you will be able to make your journey."

I was beginning to believe what Pesla was saying. We both knelt, closed our eyes, and bowed our heads. She prayed.

It was a very cold day. My feet carried me slowly for I was still very weak. There was still fog in my head. It took me a long time to reach Moscow Boulevard. But gradually my feet developed more strength, my body heated up, and I felt my old strength returning.

A wind started when I got outside the city. It developed into a real blizzard in the open field. The wind battered me from side to side. Cold penetrated through my clothes. I could barely see the road. I can hardly explain how I reached the Berzinshes not fully recovered from illness and in such foul weather. A miracle? Pesla's prayers?

Again the Berzinshes were happy to see me. They wanted to know every detail of the story from the time I had left them. Between bites of food and sips of drink I satisfied their curiosity. I ate my fill and warmed my body thoroughly. The Berzinshes had my basket filled with food for Pesla and me. I was ready for the trip back. It was already getting dark and the blizzard hadn't slackened. I decided to risk it and take the train even though that is where documents were being checked most often. On a night like this, I reasoned, the policemen might like to stay home.

The nearest station was Shkirotava. It was not long before the train to Riga arrived. People in the car were pleasant and polite. A man gave me his seat by the window. My masquerade was working again. When I walked all wrapped up, hunched, and with short little steps, I looked like an old lady. On occasion I was called grandma this or grandma that. It gave me confidence and I acted my part even more convincingly.

I made a proud grand entrance at Pesla's house. She looked at me with admiration when I uncovered the basket fully packed with food.

"It is a miracle; it is all from God. You are carrying out His commands. They must think 'up there' (a look to the ceiling) that I am a holy woman."

We got into a routine. I would keep the house, cook the meals, and stay in the big room out of sight of the neighbors. About every two weeks I would make a trip to the Berzinshes for produce.

Sometimes old women friends would come to visit Pesla. Then I stayed in the big room. I repeated again and again to her not to tell a soul about me. I could listen over the wall and hear every word spoken.

One day I heard Pesla bragging to a friend about her good fortune. ". . . God sent me a present for my old age — a daughter. She is so good to me and so handy with everything . . ." I was shaken by her words. Now the news would spread and they would come for me. I had no place else to go. My peace of mind had ended.

I visited the Berzinshes a few more times. They, too, started having a hard time to make ends meet. However, they didn't complain and filled my basket to the brim cheerfully every time. On the way back I stopped once at a new farm. I bought some potatoes, rutabagas, beets, and cottage cheese. The face of the farmer looked familiar to me. I asked him, "Are you Schusterman, the brother of Alicia?"

"Yes, and who might you be? Frida? It cannot be!"

"Yes, it is. Quite a change, isn't it?" I told him all about me.

"They are vicious animals, and our own Latvians are even worse; they try to outdo their German bosses to gain their favor. What a price to pay. I saw with my own eyes the Germans bringing in a whole train at the Rumbuli station. They were unloading Jews for hours from the freightcars into trucks. Many were already dead, frozen stiff. They were taking them to the forest where bulldozers had dug trenches. The people were lined up, undressed, at the edge, then mowed down with machine guns. The bodies were falling into the trenches. Some of them were still alive, but the bulldozers buried them. Then trucks would go for the next load until the train was empty and it was night. I cannot forget how docile all the Jews were," he said after a while. "Just a very few Germans with their Latvian helpers murdered thousands of Jews."

"They were docile because they were weakened by hunger, deprivation, and humiliation. Death was preferable to enduring more suffering. I know, I have been through the experience."

"You're probably right. It is hard to live with yourself when you see things like this going on before your very eyes and you are helpless to do anything about it. This transport must have been sent from Germany because their clothes looked different from our own."

I parted with Schusterman in a sad state of mind and returned to Pesla.

* * *

One Saturday Pesla said we must pray to God to send us a miracle of deliverance. No sooner did we get up off our knees then there was a knock on the door. I ran to the big room. For some time I heard voices but I wasn't paying attention.

Suddenly the door opened and Pesla led in a good looking, well dressed woman in her late thirties or early forties.

"This is my dear little daughter, Frida, whom I was telling you about. The angels from heaven have sent her to help me. Frida, this is Mrs. Scheink, a dear, dear friend of mine."

Mrs. Scheink ran to me and hugged and kissed me, mumbling through her tears, "My dear Fridelein, you have suffered so much, enough for your whole tribe of Israelites."

I started crying, too. It felt good to be the object of so much unexpected sympathy.

"Now, let us all pray to the Almighty, so that He may lead us in a right path to salvation," Mrs. Scheink announced in a beautiful fluent German. All three of us got to our knees. Mrs. Scheink read from the Bible and we repeated, phrase by phrase. After the prayers we rose and felt happier, as though cleansed of our troubled hearts. Before she left, Mrs. Scheink said to me:

"If you would like to do so, you may come sometimes to my house to wash some clothes. You'll have to be very careful, though, Frida. Some SS and staff officers live upstairs from us. I don't know if I should tell you this, but I provide food to two Jews, father and son. They pay me with jewelry. I was looking for a place for them to stay. They offered me a large sum. I thought of Pesla's house. Since you are here, this would be impossible. This is the will of God."

"Yes," Pesla and I agreed. We parted with hugs and kisses.

Two days passed. Late Monday evening there was a strong knock on our door. Two loud male voices: "Open the door! We come to capture the pigeon you are hiding." I thought my heart would jump out — this was it. I hid behind the door (some hiding place!). Pesla let them in.

"I don't know where she is," lied the frightened Pesla. "Maybe she went out somewhere."

The two policemen started lighting matches and looking for me in the entrance, in the kitchen, under the table, under the bed in the kitchen, in the big room. They found me.

"Come with us!"

I put on my overcoat, wrapped my face in the large farm-woven shawl. I heard Pesla praying through tears as the door closed behind us.

It was hard for me to keep up the pace of the policemen. I was scared and my knees were buckling. I am being led to execution, I was thinking.

They brought me to a police station and we entered a large room. Several policemen were there. A long table stood in the middle surrounded by chairs. A tall iron stove warmed the room, bright electric lights burned overhead, a telephone on the table. One policeman was cleaning his gun. (Ready for me?).

"Who are you and what is your name?" one police-man started interrogating me.

I decided to play a dumb farm girl. "Who, me?"

"Yes, you."

"I am a, a woman."

"Don't be funny. Open your coat."

I did. They looked at my dirty torn clothes hanging on my thin, worn body and it seemed to me that they believed me — a dumb farm girl.

"What is your name?"

"My name is Anna Schultz," I shot out without even thinking.

"How so?" one of the policemen who brought me in said with indignation. "The old lady called you some-thing else."

"Pesla thinks I am one of her daughters and calls me by a different name."

"What year were you born?"

"I don't remember."

"Don't play games. What year were you born?"

"Maybe 1905."

"Where were you born?"

"I lived in Gulbene and other places."

"I ask you where you were born, not where you lived."

"I don't know, my parents didn't tell me."

"Go and sleep on those chairs," he pointed his finger at the row of chairs by the wall. I lay down there and feigned sleep. Maybe I'd live through an-other night.

The policeman who had interrogated me started telephoning trying to get information on Anna Schultz. After a long while he called me in a loud voice: "Hey, Anna Schultz, come here."

I jumped and was in front of him, rubbing my eyes.

"Listen, could it be that you were born in Dzerbene?"

"Yes, I heard this name mentioned by my parents." There was a chance, I thought.

"Why don't you have documents?"

"I lost them."

"How can you live without food coupons?"

"I work for good people and they feed me. Sometimes one, sometimes another. I don't eat much. I am a sick girl. I throw up most of what I eat."

"Sit here. Here is a cheese sandwich," and he handed it to me. "Now eat." I ate, not even paying attention to what it was. After a while the policeman came back to me.

"First thing tomorrow morning, you go to the prefecture and get yourself a passport."

"Where shall I go for the passport?"

"I told you — to the prefecture."

"Where is the prefecture?" I played my part.

He took a piece of white paper and wrote the address of the prefecture. Then he made a map and showed me how to get there. "When you get to the prefecture tomorrow, tell them that you are Anna Schultz from Dzerbene and you have lost your passport. They will issue you a new one. Now go home."

I couldn't believe my ears. I am sure I was smiling all the way home to Pesla. I found her in the same shape as I had left her. She was on her knees by the bed praying. Her eyes were swollen from crying and her lips were mumbling something. When she saw me we fell into each other's arms and kissed and hugged and cried for some time.

"I came back from the dead," I sobbed. "It was a miracle, they let me go."

143

"I knew you would come back because I have cried and prayed to God to send you back. You see, He heard me and you are back."

I really started believing that there was something to what my dear friend said. We both fell to our knees and immersed ourselves in prayer so completely that the outside world was shut out for some time. We thanked Him for the unequalled miracles He performed to help us.

Somebody must have turned me in. People were sniffing and searching for anything suspicious to report to the police for rewards or just plain favors. It was obvious to me that I could not stay here any longer. I asked myself for the millionth time: Where to now? After much debating, I decided to go to Mrs. Scheink. Only two days before she had asked me to come and do some washing. To be sure, her house, too, was not without danger. At Pesla's, however, I could expect any day a check on whether or not I took out my passport. I was not about to stick my nose in the prefecture voluntarily.

The parting with Pesla was very touching. We had grown to love each other. She found an appropriate psalm for the occasion and on our knees we recited it and prayed to God to send us his loving kindness.

9. Frau Scheink, Olivia, the Viliumsons

Frau Scheink and her husband lived on Laimdotas Street, not far from Pesla, in a beautiful two-story mansion. She opened the door at my ring and quickly took me inside. We embraced. I told her about my arrest and miraculous release.

She let me into a small room and asked me to remove my shawl and overcoat. We both went down on our knees and I followed her words and singing. After prayer, Frau Scheink turned to me:

"Where could I hide you so my husband won't know about it? I could tell him that I hired a woman from the farm to help me with the housework, or, better, I will tell him it is only for today. What do you think?"

I had no answer.

"What kind of work can you do?" She was on the border of despair.

"I can do any kind of housework. I can also sew."

"It is good that you can do everything. The main thing is that my husband has to like you. Once we have his approval, everything will be all right."

Frau Scheink made me take a bath to rid myself of lice. I had not had a bath since I was a guest at Sonia Bobrov's apartment months ago. I looked at my thin, dried-out body — a skeleton wrapped in parchment. I felt like 90 years old. The bath was a very enjoyable experience. I lingered in it as long as I could.

Now to work, dusting, making beds, washing. I

worked fast and efficiently. The Scheinks were child-less. They lived in the lower half of the two-story house. There were many large, luxurious rooms and built-in closets for storage in every room. The bed-room and dining rooms were outfitted especially luxuriously with very expensive furniture. I found out later that this had belonged to a Jewish family who was now dead. So the Scheinks "inherited" it, so to say, and owned it . . .

For the night, Frau Scheink hid me in the base-ment. It felt good to have a full stomach for a change and to sleep fearlessly for a night.

In the morning Frau Scheink dressed me in a little white cap and apron and put me in front of a sewing machine in the entryroom to stitch her husband's shirts and underwear. Hour after hour passed with this work.

Suddenly a neighbor SS officer came in.

"Guten Tag, gnädige Frau," click with the heels. "Is Herr Scheink in?"

My hands were shaking, but I appeared to pay no attention.

"Nein, mein Herr," Mrs. Scheink politely replied. "He will be here in the afternoon. I will tell him that you looked for him and he'll pay you a visit."

"Danke schön, Madam," he clicked his heels again and was gone.

"You are lucky you didn't turn around." Mrs. Scheink put her arms around my shoulders. "This SS officer teaches other officers how to recognize Jews by their facial structure and eye expression."

"Why then have you put me here in such a con-spicuous place, where everyone entering can see me?"

"My dear Frida, I know a little how people think. Here you are in full view and nobody is going to pay attention to you. If somebody catches a glimpse of you in a far-away room, they will immediately be curious as to who you are."

"This makes sense. You are very clever, Frau Scheink, but it did give me a scare."

I spent three nights in the basement. Mr. Scheink knew already that I worked in the house, but he did not know that I slept in the basement.

Mr. Scheink worked in the city in an office. He was not an Adventist, but neither was he a Nazi. He maintained cordial relations with his SS officer neighbors, but did not participate in their nightly drunken parties.

Mrs. Scheink could not hold back any longer and told her husband all about me. At first he wasn't very pleased and would give me suspicious glances. However, seeing how diligently I worked, how spotlessly I maintained the house, how white his shirts were laundered — all this free — he softened. He even arranged for Mrs. Scheink to make a bed for me in a back room in the house.

Good things don't last. One morning Mrs. Scheink came out of her bedroom pale and upset: "Frida my darling, I am afraid you will not be able to stay with us any longer. My husband cannot sleep at night. He is afraid someone will find you here. I will try to find you another place."

The same day she went to the other side of the River Dvina to contact friends about a place for me to stay, but she returned depressed. None of her friends wanted to take the risk. The next day she did the same thing, with the same results.

Sunday made a week since I had come to live with the Scheinks. A young German girl came to visit Mrs. Scheink. She was tall and thin, blond hair and very pretty. She spoke German in a very perky, fast manner. She radiated youthfulness, energy, and good humor. Mrs. Scheink was very glad to see her.

"Olivia darling, I am so glad to see you. Now during the war we don't visit as often. How is the family?"

"They are all fine. I had some business to do for Papa in the city, so I thought I would drop in to see you for a moment."

"Olivia, this is Frida. She is Jewish and is hiding out in our house." She told her all about me. Olivia looked me over skeptically as if she did not believe what she heard.

"You live on a farm," I said to her. "Could I stay with you for a couple of weeks, maybe? I can sew very well. I could make you a coat that would really enhance your beauty, I can promise you that."

"All right, Frida, but let's not walk together. Follow me and keep a distance of about a block. If you should be stopped and detained, you are on your own."

"I will do that."

"Can you walk? We have about 25 kilometers to make today."

"When it comes to staying alive, I can walk over 100 kilometers."

"I have to make one more visit in the city; from there we'll go straight home."

We parted with Frau Scheink. I thanked her for her many favors and kindnesses and we embraced like old friends.

Olivia walked quickly with a youthful gait, but I easily matched her with my long experience in walking. She entered a house on Artillery Street 17; I did the same. We entered an apartment together, without talking to each other. Here two of Olivia's friends

148

lived, Sasha and Greta. Olivia told them about me and the two girls listened with great compassion.

"Do not worry," they assured me, seeing my uneasiness, "We won't tell a soul. On the contrary, we'll pray to God for you and for your speedy salvation." They, too, were strict Adventists.

We had a long way ahead of us, so we did not stay there long. Again we were out on the street, Olivia in front and I following. We crossed downtown, then the bridge across the Dvina River and on to the Bauskas Highway where we stopped. The road was empty of traffic. Then I saw a little black dot in the distance. As it came nearer it turned out to be a peasant driving a horse and sleigh.

Olivia stayed in the middle of the road and asked for a ride. The peasant paid no attention to her and passed by. As he did so, she sprinted after the sleigh and jumped in the back. Seeing this, I, too, started running to overtake the sleigh. My heart was beating so fast I thought it would leap out of my chest. A little more effort and I jumped into the sleigh, too. The peasant was aware we were there but didn't even turn around. I caught my breath. We did not talk, didn't even look at each other, as though we were together by accident.

We rode like this for about 15 kilometers until we came to a fork in the road. Olivia jumped off the sleith easily while I rode on a little and then jumped off, too. The farmer still kept riding without turning around. I ran to Olivia.

"We have only about 7 more kilometers left. On this road we cannot hope for a ride; very few people come through here. We'll have to walk." The road led through fields, a forest, some snow-covered marshes, more fields and there, on top of a hill, a house.

"That is our house," Olivia announced with pride in her voice. "It is very peaceful and beautiful here."

What a paradise — I was thinking — so many places to hide. The forest, the haystacks, the hills, the hollows, the holes in the ground; it is lucky I came here.

Olivia led me into the house. Her old mother was there. She gave me an unkind look as though saying, "What kind of a beauty did you bring to us this time?"

Olivia took her mother aside and they started talking in whispers. In the meantime Olivia's father came in — a man of about 70, tall, with a long, white fluffy beard like Santa Claus. He joined Olivia and her mother. They talked excitedly in whispers. I could see that an argument was going on having to do with me. Olivia was trying to pacify her mother. Her father was showing restraint. Finally they agreed to keep me for two weeks. (Thanks for that.) Officially I would be their guest for two weeks.

Their name was Viliumson. I found out later that the Viliumsons, the Scheinks, Pesla, and Sasha and Gerta all belonged to the same Seventh Day Adventist sect.

The Viliumsons' house consisted of one big room together with the kitchen. In the middle of the room stood a vertical tree log that supported a low ceiling. Two small windows supplied the light. Potted plants adorned the windowsills. A brick oven and cook stove combination marked the kitchen, with copper kettles and pans hanging from nails on the wall. A side door led into a room made of plywood, which was used only in summer, Olivia explained. It was cold there now, as cold as outside. This room had one large window. Through it one could see a neighbor's house. It looked quite rich with a large barn, stalls, and many stacks of hay.

When it got dark the Viliumsons had a religious service with the traditional Adventist evening prayers. Afterwards there was dinner and then bed.

The next morning I studied thoroughly the layout of the Viliumson house. I did this so that if the time came I had to hide, I would be prepared. The Viliumsons warned me that it might happen that a policeman or other official would suddenly ride up on a bicycle to bring information on new rules, laws, or decrees. Neighbors, too, might look in once in a while. It would be good for me to stay out of sight so as not to arouse curiosity and suspicion. They did have a small dog, but she wasn't much use — she slept under the table most of the time. She would start barking only after a stranger was already in the house.

I started making good on my promise to Olivia of making her an overcoat. The design and fit were excellent. It hid Olivia's thin frame. Everybody liked it. Now her father and mother wanted coats, too.

I was glad they liked my work and wanted more. I promised to fill their order. My work, however, did not progress smoothly. I was often interrupted by the visits of neighbors, especially one neighbor's little five-year-old boy, Liulik. The reason for secrecy was that we wished to delay knowledge of my presence for as long as possible; it would look strange for a guest from the city to remain longer than two weeks with a poor family such as the Viliumsons. So I went into hiding any time we saw or heard anyone coming. We could not bolt the door, either. Doors of farmhouses were always unlocked, and people, especially neighbors, seldom knocked. Anything different would rouse suspicion.

My two weeks at the Viliumsons had long passed. Mother Viliumson was grumbling more and more about how hard it was to make ends meet. I understood myself that an extra mouth to feed was a burden to them. They had a garden, one cow, several chickens. From this they had to make some deliveries to the German authorities.

One evening the whole family started to discuss what to do with me. Not only was I a burden because of food, but my long stay might not be too healthy either. Mother Viliumson suggested consulting her younger son, Hein (short for Heinrich), who lived about 9 kilometers away in Kekava. Next morning Olivia went to see her brother. She told him all about me. Hein was very moved and returned with Olivia to have a look at me himself.

"This is God's will," he intoned to his parents. "It is His will that she live. If we don't save her we will be committing a grave sin, a sin for which the whole family is responsible. All our lives we will have to live with this sin. There is no atonement for it . . ."

There was a long silence, each of us absorbed in his own thoughts.

"I will give you what amounts to Frida's keep," Hein said. "We can manage that. Edith will go along with that."

It was decided that I would stay on with the Viliumsons. I was amazed by Hein's heated arguments. They were all deeply religious people. The Adventists had an especially soft spot for Israelites, God's chosen people.

Hein was as handsome as the rest of the Viliumsons. He worked in Kekava as a miller and was well off. He and his wife, Edith, had no children.

* * *

Days and weeks passed. The winter cold had lifted some in March. The days were sunny and warm. The snow was melting in the daytime and freezing at night. Long, beautiful icicles had formed all around the edge of the roof. I dared not go outside in the beckoning sunshine because our neighbors had been told that I had returned to Riga sometime ago.

The spring was a very unpleasant time of year for Olivia. She was like a beautiful apple on the outside, eaten through by a worm inside, She had tuberculosis. She was often given to long fits of coughing and occasionally was spitting up blood. Her breathing came hard with a wheezing sound in her chest. Olivia was very neat and clean and guarded others from contamination. She took various pills and medicines to ease her condition. My heart ached for her. In a short time we had become very close friends. I gladly took on all her chores in the house. I washed the wooden floors until they gleamed, dusted everything, cleaned in all the corners and helped Mother Viliumson in the kitchen with all the hard work. I brought in water from the well late at night. The well was near the forest, a distance from the house. It took three trips with two buckets each to satisfy our daily needs. The uphill walk with the two buckets of water and slipping noiselessly by the neighbors wasn't easy.

It was warm enough now to hide in the summer room. I cleaned it thoroughly and did all the sewing there, but had to be quiet when visitors came.

The Viliumsons had an older son, Kurt. He was married to a Latvian girl, Ruti, and they lived in Riga where Kurt worked as an orderly in a hospital. One day they came to visit. The Viliumsons of course told Kurt about me, in secret from his wife. He was quite upset with the situation.

"Who are we to play hero and risk our heads for a — a Jewess? I beg you, if your lives mean anything to you, tell her to leave. She'll find other good-hearted people."

He argued with his parents to no avail, and he left unhappy, tense, almost angry. Nothing changed in the arrangement about me.

Early in April the weather turned warm, time to work in the fields. For the benefit ᴏ̣ the neighbors I came back again from Riga for a visit and to help with the spring planting.

Olivia taught me how to spread manure evenly over the ground. Then came ploughing. I did a very poor job at first. The plough was too heavy; the horse would lead me into a crooked furrow, but I did not give up. I clenched my teeth and, wet with perspiration, I held the plough handles with all my strength. Gradually the horse started following my commands and my hands acquired skill handling the plough. My furrows grew straight now, which made me really proud. I was so tired by evening I almost crawled home, but I was happy and contented.

After the soil preparation came the sowing of rye, the planting of potatoes, beets, carrots, and other vegetables. The Viliumsons also had a small greenhouse near the forest. Tomato plants were raised there to about a quarter of a meter high. This greenhouse served me as a handy hiding place. I would run to it whenever a stranger approached the Viliumson property. In the greenhouse I somehow felt out of danger. I worked in it with great pleasure. It wasn't hard for me to carry 40 buckets of water every day to water my children, the young plants.

One time I got caught in the Viliumsons house by several visitors from a neighboring village. I was introduced as a friend of Mother Viliumson, belonging to the same Adventist sect.

"How can you avoid working for the Germans? You are so young and beautiful," one of the peasants asked.

"I am not well and was freed from work," I answered.

It showed that we had to be more careful. Here on the farm each new person is noticed immediately. I would have to stay out of sight and reappear only for short periods, as a guest. The danger lay in not having any kind of documents and in not being registered. This would be the first thing anybody would look for and ask about.

During the summer it was much easier to stay in hiding — nature herself hid me from my enemies. During the day I did my sewing and at night I slept hidden in a stack of hay.

The Viliumsons had a permit to mow hay in the forest. I spent the greater part of the summer there. I learned to cut hay, dry it, stack it — I loved it. Father Viliumson and Olivia used to come often to work in the forest. They would stay and work until noon and then depart, while I stayed on to wander around and collect mushrooms and berries. With nightfall I would climb in one of the haystacks to sleep. So passed summer until the rains of fall. Now began a time of hard work with the harvest. Again I surfaced for the neighbors' benefit as though coming back from Riga to help with the harvest.

The whole family was now in the field digging potatoes, beets, carrots, onions, etc. Even Kurt and his wife came from Riga to help. This was his first visit since winter. He was afraid of informers and possible catastrophe. Now, however, he was more relaxed, seeing that my presence was not so dangerous after all, and how much benefit his family was deriving from

155

my work. Besides, I was taking part in the prayers and religious observances, and this was very important to him — acquiring a "lost soul." However, Kurt was very careful and distant. He spoke to me only when he really had to. To his wife, Ruti, I was a Latvian girl from Riga, a friend of Olivia's who visited occasionally. Ruti wanted me to do some sewing for her, but Kurt stepped in and talked her out of it. She obediently followed his every wish. They left after a few days.

Another winter was approaching and with it new problems. What was to be done with me during the winter months?

Olivia traveled to the city just about every day canvassing her friends for a place for me to stay. Everyone was afraid to take on the danger. Hein and Edith finally suggested that I live with them for a while in Kekava. I would have to stay in hiding all the time and do some sewing for them. One evening Hein came for me with his horse and took me back to his village.

Hein and Edith lived on the second floor of a two-story wooden house. A few other German military families lived there, too. Our apartment had two rooms with one door out in the corridor. There in the corridor was also the communal lavatory for all the people on the floor.

The environs of the village of Kekava were very beautiful. It looked like a landscape an artist of the German/Dutch school would paint. In the center of the village was the grain mill powered by a waterfall. All around were large, rich farmhouses in the midst of greenery and flowers. In the summer it must be heavenly, I thought. This, of course, is good for people who have a right to live, not for me . . .

Edith was very good to me. She was trying hard to

fatten me up. Being a very good cook, the house was always filled with savory aromas which I was just sponging up. They had an abundance of flour, of course, with which one could buy anything. It was a commodity more precious than money. Edith baked all kinds of fancy breads and other delicacies. My favorite was pancakes made with sour milk and stuffed with preserves. On this kind of diet my body filled out and began to take on a youthful look. My skin lost the parchment color and within a few weeks appeared not nearly so old.

I still lived in fear. The main problem was going to the community toilet in the corridor. Before every trip I listened carefully for any sign of life in the hall. Then I ventured out, quiet as a mouse. The same procedure was followed on the way back. Most of the time Edith went out on reconnaissance and would signal me to venture out. She would stay on guard until I was through. Sometimes it took an hour or more of waiting until the coast was clear.

Most of my time was spent sewing clothes for Edith. She had many pieces of material.

A couple of weeks passed in comparative peace and quiet. One day there came a knock. I ran immediately to hide in the wardrobe as we had decided on. Edith locked it and took the key. I lay there quietly like I was dead in a coffin. I could hear everything going on outside. It turned out that this was Edith's brother. He had volunteered in the army and came to say goodbye.

"Why you have to thrust yourself into the very heat of battle, by your own free will, is beyond me to understand," his sister argued.

"If everyone thought like you, then who would fight the Bolsheviks?"

"All I know is that war, any war, is immoral and against the will of God," came Hein's voice.

"You ought to be ashamed of yourselves speaking like you do. To let others do the fighting for you and you reap the rewards."

"Fighting for what?" Hein asked.

"Fighting to free the world of Jews and Communists, fighting for an Aryan master world, fighting for the Führer and Latvia." His voice was shrill now, and they quieted him down by saying, "Well, it's your affair. You are old enough to have your own opinion. We couldn't help expressing ours."

"I fear for your life. You are my brother. I love you. Do be careful," Edith said.

The whole day passed in endless talk and argument. Edith's brother told boisterous stories about his drinking parties, how popular he was with the girls, that there wasn't a girl who refused to sleep with him, that in the New Germany religious marriage was going to be done away with . . . and on and on.

I had my troubles — I needed to relieve myself badly but dared not move and barely breathed. I prayed not to cough or sneeze as happened in so many stories where people lost their lives that way.

Late that night the brother decided to leave. Edith opened the wardrobe. "You still alive there?" I shot out the door like a bullet into the lavatory, all precautions forgotten. Luck was with me, I made it safely.

My stay with Hein and Edith came to an end. We had planned it to last a month for it would be too dangerous for me to stay longer in one place.

Olivia came for me. Sasha and Greta Kleibais agreed to let me stay with them in Riga. It didn't take me long to pack and we were on the way.

The Kleibaises lived with their old father in a

three-room community apartment on the fourth floor. The kitchen was for the common use of several apartment dwellers. So was the toilet located on a platform between two flights of stairs.

The father, despite his advanced age, was in good health, liked his schnapps and good food. He was a little drunk most of the time and always in a good mood for a joke and a laugh. I was introduced to him as Anna, a Latvian friend.

Greta worked as a nurse in a military hospital, while Sasha was a cook in another hospital for tuberculosis patients. In the morning, Sasha and Greta would get their father off to work, then they would leave, locking the door. I stayed alone in the large apartment and did some sewing. My art of sewing made me welcome in all the places I stayed, and here was no exception. Not all the tenants left during the day. I had to be careful as before in making trips to the lavatory. By now I was quite experienced and used to living with this inconvenience. But here it was more complicated. The toilet was half a flight of stairs down, so I had to wait until there was no traffic on our floor and on the floor below. Sometimes it took hours to watch for such a moment.

One day a knock on the door sent me hiding under a bed. An aunt of my friends had come to visit. I was listening: "Aunt Margarete, how good of you to come. Why all in black?" Greta greeted her.

"Children, I received word that Erick was captured by the Russians. We can only expect the worst. I cry my eyes out and spend most of the day in prayer."

"I thought he was a staff officer and not on the front," Greta continued the conversation.

"Sit down, Aunt Margarete, I'll go in the kitchen and make some tea. We also have some kuchen left from a birthday party." This was Sasha, always thinking of something to eat.

"The news is bad," Aunt Margarete continued. "You heard, no doubt, what is going on on the Stalingrad front. Bloody battles are taking place. They are fighting fiercely for every little piece of ground." She sighed gravely. "The casualties are heavy. Who knows if we are being told the whole truth? Only God knows how all this will end."

"Yes, dear. I know it at first hand from my patients in the hospital. They say there is a real slaughterhouse and what the Russians cannot accomplish the winter does. I have many patients with gangrene from frostbite. They bring in people half rotten, and what a smell — it is a horror to see."

I heard the clatter of glasses, spoons mixing, compliments for the cake. Someone turned on the radio — mournful music wafted through the rooms as if a funeral was going on. To me it meant that salvation was that much closer. Their misfortune was my good news. I was happy that things started turning the worse for Hitler. I was glad my friends could not read my thoughts or feel my heart. They were German in the marrow of their bones and the defeats to them were not defeats for Hitler and what he stood for, but defeat for Germans and Germany. It was their personal honor, their loyalty to the German nation, that made them feel the hurt, though they were truly pacifists by religious conviction.

The women started praying passionately to the all-powerful Lord. They called to the Heavens with loud supplication to His justice and fairness for their brothers suffering at the front. On this point I could not agree with my benefactors. I, too, prayed, lying there under the bed, for the total defeat of Germany, the Nazis, and Hitler.

I knew very little of what was going on in the outside world. I seldom had a chance to read the papers or listen to the radio. My information came from snatches of overheard conversations, occasional glimpses at old newspapers, once in a while a newscast on the radio which was turned on by my friends (never by me).

I worked at the Kleibaises on Artillery Street for six weeks. Olivia came for me then and took me to still another place for one more winter month — Edith's parents. Olivia told them who I was of course, so they would know what they were in for. She praised my sewing skills to them and promised that I would make first-class garments for them.

Edith's parents, the Goertners, lived on the other side of the River Dvina in a little wooden house. It consisted of two rooms and a kitchen. And wonder of wonders, the toilet was inside the house — what luck!

On the other side of the house, in a room with a separate entrance, lived Edith's sister, Bruni. She was a young, vivacious fräulein who had already managed to have a child by a German soldier. She worked somewhere and was continually troubled by her restless child that she was bringing over for her mother to take care of. With the same family also lived Edith's grandfather, a white-haired, handsome, dignified old man.

I spent the whole month sewing clothes for the entire family — overcoats, dresses, suits. These required alterations from clothes taken from the luckless Jews and distributed to the general population. I winced every time I picked up another garment. Who had it belonged to before? There were men's suits, children's garments, women's blouses, skirts, even party dresses.

Edith's mother was very nice to me. She liked my

work very much. She would often come to sit by me and talk.

"It is good our son joined the army," she once said. "You could not have stayed had he been here. He had his nasty friends around all the time, drinking, wenching, cursing . . . Children of the same mother — the boy a Fascist Nazi, the daughter hiding out a Jewess . . ."

"This is how the world is," I said, "Friends and enemies, men and animals often come from the same womb, fed the same mother's milk . . ."

"Yes, yes, you are right, my dear," she sighed gravely. "I am ashamed of my boy . . ."

My work came to an end. All the extra food was gone, too. I decided to go back to the Viliumsons in Katlakalns. I walked all the way by myself and waited in the forest until night came, then quietly entered the friendly house. They had been expecting me to show up any day. I stayed in hiding until spring came, then emerged as if I had just come from the city to visit and help with the spring chores.

If something persists long enough, one gets used to it and learns to live with it. So it was with my constant fear of being caught. Sometimes I thought the Viliumsons had calmed down and lost sight of the dangers that lurked all around us.

We were sitting around the table one evening after supper. Kurt walked in; he had come from Riga. He was sullen, barely kissed his mother, and announced: "I bring bad news. There are rumors in the city that the Viliumsons are hiding a Jewess."

Nobody said anything for a long time. I thought all eyes were focused on me as though saying "You hold our lives in your hands, have pity, leave."

"I will leave immediately," I said, getting up, "and not subject my best friends to danger."

162

"We will pack you some food," Mama Viliumson said and started preparing my well-worn basket. I overheard Olivia whispering to her father while Kurt was with his mother in the kitchen: "We must not lose such a person. Whatever you say, she is holy, a saved soul. This is God's miracle."

"What can we do? What if they come and find her here — all of us will perish. There isn't much choice . . ."

We prayed together with tears in everyone's eyes and started to say our goodbyes.

"Where will you go?" Mother Viliumson asked with sympathy in her voice.

"I will wander in the nearby forests. I may find some other good people like you whom I can stay with for a while." I was speaking as though I was sure of myself, as though I had definite plans, which I hadn't. There was no need to make them feel bad — my best, my only true friends in this world.

I went to the forest. The magnificent tall pines enveloped me. It gave me a feeling of freedom and spaciousness. Besides, every tree, bush, hole offered a hiding place. I ran, danced, even turned a somersault. Had anyone seen me he would have thought I had gone crazy.

When darkness came I went quietly to the Viliumsons' back yard and hid in a haystack for the night. In about an hour I heard someone climbing up to me — Olivia! Her father was standing below.

"Come down," she said, "come back into the house."

"Why?" I asked.

"When you left, Father and I started reading the Bible. Our conscience was tearing us to pieces — had we really done the right thing? We kept on reading and came to a psalm, and it all became clear to us —

God, our Lord, wanted to test us, to find out how well we understood Him and follow His teachings, how strong our faith was. Therefore, He sent us His chosen Anna to test us with fear."

"The Lord is all powerful," Mr. Viliumson intoned. "We should not question His ways. The enemy is powerless in His presence, he cannot hear or see what is passing right in front of him and therefore, he will not notice you, if He so wills it."

They spoke with such fervor, such ardor, such burning faith and emotion that I, too, was caught up in the spirit — I was on my knees with my eyes lifted to the dark, star-studded sky with tears of gratitude running down my cheeks. Never again in my life have I experienced such deep emotion, such unquestioning faith, such human goodness as radiated from those two figures in the dark.

The Viliumsons were true practicing Adventists. Every line and every interpretation of the Bible was observed without question. Everything depended on the loving kindness of the Lord. If God wills it, then nothing bad can happen. This was their conclusion, and it calmed everyone.

I stayed with the Viliumsons. Of course, I was even more careful than before. The forest was my home, really. In summer time it was much better there than staying in the house. Less dangerous, too. Most of the days I spent collecting mushrooms and picking berries, and at night sleeping in a haystack.

I seldom went into their house, only on occasion joined them in prayer. We all knelt, sang hymns and psalms in praise and adoration of the Lord our God, extolling His justice, His miracles, His wonders.

My thoughts were gnawing my innards — Dear God, how long will You make me pray in an alien faith, when will my tortures end, when will You free me?

I was thinking about my dear ones — my mother, my sisters. Could it be that some of them were still alive? It is not very likely. If they did survive, they, too, would be in doubt about my survival. I wanted to live so very much . . . If I could only live to tell about the murderous deeds visited upon our people, then it would not be so terrifying to die. I felt an obligation to fulfill, an obligation to my friends, to my people who were wiped out without a trace, and only I remained to tell of their fate.

The times of prayer — those were the times of my gravest thoughts. I really did pray, my own way.

To my mind came a conversation with Olivia: "In your place, Anna, I would rather have let them shoot me than having to go through the ordeal of suffering and fear. What is life? What do we need it for? I will tell it straight, I don't value it at all. It is like a cheap present. It is only a temporary existence in preparation for the 'real life,' which lasts forever. One had to spend all his present life to prepare for his everlasting 'real life.'"

"How can you say such a thing — cheap present? The way I was taught is that life is the most precious gift of God. It is to be valued, guarded, and cherished most ardently. God has given us one life. He has also given us the freedom of choice to do good or evil and He will judge us by what path we take."

"You speak like a holy person. Papa says you are. You make me ashamed of what I just said."

"I am no holy person. I am just a leaf blown about by the wind. Sometimes I am up in the air, then thrown to the ground. As for what you said, you have nothing to be ashamed of, my dear friend. There is so much goodness and sincerity in you. You have made me love you like a sister, like my own flesh and blood."

"I always thought that this life on earth was just a stopping place, an interlude, for life in Heaven to come, which will be a life of goodness, of joy and eternity."

"It may be as you say, but we don't know that for sure. What we do know is that we are alive, here, on earth, now, and God is watching us from above and judging us for what we do, what we think, and how we manage our lives. He has created us and given us life and the world we live in for our domain. We must be thankful for this most cherished of all gifts."

* * *

In the middle of the summer I once came to visit the Viliumson house after a long stay in the forest. A girl from the neighboring farm came to visit Olivia. Her name was Emilia. They talked for a while. Then Olivia said to her, "I want to show you some clothes that Anna made." She got out all the finery I had made for her and spread it out for her friend to see.

Emilia started fingering the nicely gathered folds, the delicate hemstitching of the collars and sleeves enviously. She oh'ed and ah'ed.

"Anna is free now," Olivia said. "If you want, she can go to work for you for a while. I know you have a sewing machine."

"Oh, that would be wonderful. I am sure Mama will agree. She has many pieces of material she tucked away in her wardrobe for years. It is all settled, then?"

In a couple of days Emilia came for me, and we left for the neighboring farm.

Emilia lived with her mother and brother on a very rich farm. They had two houses, one old one where they lived and the other still abuilding. The new house still had a dirt floor and the interior trim was missing, otherwise it was finished. They had a lot of land, cows, horses, swine, chickens, ducks.

Emilia's family knew about me from the Viliumsons — that I was Olivia's Latvian girl friend from Riga and that I had a permit not to work for the Germans because of my ill health.

I asked them to keep my presence on their farm quiet because if the Germans found out that I was working I could lose my work exemption permit. They agreed. We all decided that I should do my work and live in the new house because nobody went there. If there was a search, I would have plenty of building material around to hide in. There were stacks of boards, sheets of plywood, beams and boxes of hardware.

I went to work almost immediately, chose styles, took measurements, and cut up material. It was a pleasure to work here in solitude, with a full stomach, in the new building with the resin smell of the freshly cut lumber. Thus I worked from morning until night, as long as daylight lasted.

My hosts were kind to me. They brought food three times a day and always inquired if I needed something else. So it went day after day.

Emilia's brother was a bachelor nearing forty. He suddenly started coming to visit me often, always bringing with him something pleasant like a half-open rosebud, a piece of cake, a few extra cubes of sugar (very scarce those days). He also never missed an occasion to compliment me on how straight and fast I walked, my figure, my face — he admired everything. It was obvious that he was courting me. One day he opened up: "Anna, I thought a long time about this, I observed you and I like you very much. It would be a good thing if you and I got married. I am a good man."

I was hoping against hope that I would be finished with my work before it came to this. I had seen it coming and now it was here. What to do, what to say?

"Anton, you flatter me very much and I respect your feelings, but the match would not be good for you for many reasons. It is because I am so grateful to you and your family for taking me in, giving me work, being so nice to me that I am going to tell you a few things you don't know about me."

"I don't care about your past; you need not tell me. I know you are a good woman and I would like to have you for my wife."

"Hear me out, Anton. You are a big, strong, handsome man. You have quite a lot of land, livestock, fowl, timber. You need a strong, healthy woman who can manage such a large, rich household. I am a sick woman and have not long to live [I had never been sick in my life]. Never mind how I look outwardly, inside I am dying a little bit every day. Why do you think I am here, a master fashion designer, a tailor and seamstress? I am here for the fresh air, the sunshine, to prolong my life a few weeks, a few months. It would be selfish and unkind of me not to have told you, to marry you knowing that in a short time you would be a widower."

"I had no way of knowing, Anna. I appreciate your honesty. Now I respect you even more. I will do everything I can to make your stay here more pleasant. You are right about our marrying. We can be good friends, though."

He left, saddened. His attention to me did not end, however. It took on a different character. His visits

168

were more like visits to an ailing friend, and the awkward relationship between us ceased.

One day I heard the noise of several motorcycles. I quickly hid my work, the machine, and myself in a prearranged place, masked off with lumber. I was almost certain that this was a search for me. Somebody must have betrayed my presence here. After a while, I heard the door open and Emilia's composed voice saying, "Please come in and search. You will see we are hiding no one."

I could see through a crack. One SS man came in, gave a quick look all around and left. I could breathe again. Is this one more of those tests God was subjecting me to and showing me His strong hand? I could not but believe that this was one more miracle. He wanted me to stay alive.

Later Emilia came in. She told me that the Germans were looking for deserters and were quite put out about it. They were making searches of every farm and suspected even their own SS men.

This was good news. It meant that the Germans were not doing so well.

A few days after the search I finished my work and returned to the Viliumsons. Emilia and her mother gave me some money, a few kilograms of butter and other food. I turned this all over to Mama Viliumson. After greeting them, having a meal, and saying prayers, I went back to the forest. There was a lot of work to be done cutting hay on the Viliumson plot. It felt good to do physically strenuous work and be in the open air. The forest always gave me a sense of freedom and security.

In the evening I was quite tired. I climbed up on one of the haystacks, ate my black bread and sour milk and sank into a sweet restful sleep. Something woke me. I lifted my head and looked down. I saw a figure running as fast as he could over the field and nearing the forest. It was a young man. He hid in a neighboring stack of hay. He must have been a deserter. Now I understood the roundups and searches of the SS men. I was overjoyed — the Germans apparently weren't having everything their own way anymore; they must be having troubles.

The Latvians stopped believing everything the Nazis said on the radio; they started being discriminating when listening to the news and began reading between the lines of the propaganda. There were no more volunteers, and the Latvians were avoiding the draft by hiding out in the forests, in cellars and bunkers. "The rats are leaving the sinking ship," ran through my mind. Maybe, maybe soon . . .

Later the same night I heard a woman's voice calling softly, "A-oo-oo-oo, A-oo-oo-oo, A-oo-oo-oo (the call for recognition in the forest)." I was again on the alert. Two figures met, one handed the other a package, they stood a while, then parted. One figure went across the field toward the farms, the other disappeared into the forest. This kind of scene was repeated many times in the last few weeks. Deserters. Good.

* * *

On Saturday, I usually came home to the Viliumsons. This was the holy day, the Sabbath. They would spend the day in prayer, fasting, and resting. They prayed and fasted for the Germans who fell in battle and at the same time for those who perished from the Fascist atrocities, and they prayed to ward off calamities befalling family and friends.

I tried as best I could to follow their customs, rules, and way of life so as to become one of them.

The household management came to a halt Saturdays. Rest and peace reigned. The cow, however, being a living creature, had to be fed, milked, and taken to pasture. I took it upon myself to perform this chore even though it was "sinful" to do so. While thus engaged I would temporarily break the fast with a little milk and a raw egg occasionally. Afterwards, however, my conscience bothered me because I thought the Viliumsons suspected me of not being as devout as I should be.

I was reasoning to myself that it would be hypocritical to fast for the fallen German soldiers or the German adversities. After all, this was an alien faith for me. I did follow the family customs in order not to hurt their feelings. I worked very hard all week long and did not intend to fast on the day of rest. I did not eat out in the open. Usually, I kept in my coat pocket a piece of dried bread, dry cheese, a carrot or other food that would keep well. This was intended for other unforeseen situations as well as for Saturday. Mama Viliumson found my coat on the haystack when she went to feed the cow. She told the family about it pleasantly enough and in my presence when she returned to the house. I felt uneasy and didn't know how to handle the matter.

"I do this so that in case of an emergency when I have to run into hiding, I won't be totally without food," I said.

"You are smart, my child. We don't mind, just keep on doing it and you won't go hungry."

A person who has eaten feels guilty knowing those near him have been fasting. It is possible that they sensed my indiscretion and said nothing.

One time, Olivia showed me a place in the Holy Scriptures where it said that a stranger in their society need not follow all the prohibitions and restrictions of the sect, such as resting, or fasting. I felt awkward and uncomfortable — she knew. She wanted to put me at ease, my dear Olivia. She had a sixth sense, penetrating my moods and feelings. Somehow she understood my hidden passion to be with my own, to pray in my own faith. She was tolerant of my lacks in observing their sect's canons.

*   *   *

July and August was the season for berries; then after the rains started came the season for mushrooms. These were my happiest times. Day after day, Olivia and I would go deep into the thickest part of the forest where nobody came and reap a bounty. We would come home with heavy baskets filled with the gifts of the forest. There was enough for everybody and everything: for selling in the city, for preserves, for gifts. We made pleasant surprise presents for Madam Scheink, Sasha and Greta, and also Pesla. Of course, they didn't tell Pesla about me because she couldn't be trusted not to give me away.

I never dared go too deeply into the forest myself for fear of getting lost. Olivia suggested once doing that because the berries were more plentiful there.

"I don't know the road too well myself," she said, "so I invited Martha to go with us. She knows the forest better than the animals that live there." Martha was a girl from a neighboring farm. I had met her before at the Viliumsons. She was an Adventist, too, and she took me as one of the family.

We walked for a long time far into the forest. Then we started picking the fruit. There was such an abundance of berries that our baskets were full in no time. As I came near my friends, I tripped and fell over something, spilling some of my berries. It turned out

172

to be a small spade such as the military was using, but minus a handle. I called to Olivia and showed her what I had found.

"What does this mean?" I asked.

"Keep it and hide it. It may come in handy some day," Olivia said, looking the spade over.

"What do I need it for?"

"Just hide it, why not? It doesn't cost you a thing."

"All right, I'll take it with me. Maybe we could use it."

This spade saved my life a year later.

We came home with heavy baskets full to the brim with wild strawberries, blackberries, and raspberries. As we neared the house on the hill, we could see that the Germans were installing large projectors not far from the highway.

"What is that for?" I asked.

"They light up the sky with these to seek out the Red planes flying over at night," Olivia explained.

"It's odd that they have erected those projectors right here. There are no military objectives or German military troops stationed here."

"Just because there are no military objectives here it is more advantageous to have them here since we are twenty-five kilometers from Riga and they can defend the city better from here."

I was elated: the Germans have to defend Riga! But of course I kept it to myself.

One evening after prayers, I was climbing my haystack for the night when the whole sky suddenly lit up as bright as if it were day. It looked as though hundreds of blinding lamps were suspended over the earth.

What could this mean? I asked myself. Are the Reds coming? My heart beat fast from excitement. I was barely holding back my great joy at seeing this night spectacle and waiting for a miracle. There came a roar from planes which started releasing bombs producing an ear-splitting whistle as they fell, then exploding all around us — in the forest, in the fields, one very close to the Urkevich farm, our neighbors. The next day we went around looking at the bomb craters and collecting bomb fragments. I was sorry that the Red planes had not found a better place to bomb. The pilots apparently were disoriented by all the lights and thought it to be a good target.

The whole village was frightened by the bombardment. Most of the people lay flat on the ground away from their houses. Some cried, others prayed, all expected the bomb which would take them to the Netherworld. On the contrary, I was not frightened. These bombs were bombs of salvation. I'd rather have died from a Russian bomb than from a German gun. I was waiting for the Red Army to show itself after all this. How naïve I was; how little I knew about such things. When the bombers left, everything went back to the usual daily routine. The projectors, however, stayed put. They drilled the night sky with their long shafts of light in search of Russian planes.

My expectations were premature. Days were passing without signs of war or battles.

Hein and Edith came to see us and to find out how we had fared during the bombardment. They stayed a couple of days and asked me to go with them to Kekava for a while. Edith had received several packages of clothes from her mother — left over by Jews. These people had all been killed, and I was asked to remake these garments for Edith and Hein, as I had done for Edith's mother in Riga. The work was not hard or demanding, but it was depressing every time

174

I picked up a new piece. It could have belonged to one of my friends . . . I tried to chase these thoughts from my mind but they kept returning like persistent flies.

I felt imprisoned in their house. I couldn't go out; I could only sew, eat, rest. Edith fed me well as before, the best of everything. She was always inventing new dishes and made a pleasure out of eating. I gained strength and weight. I was in a happy mood because of the Nazi defeats which couldn't be hidden any longer, and the prospect of my liberation.

Hein and Edith were happy over another matter. Edith was pregnant. They had been married six years and this would be their first child. Edith asked me to make some maternity clothes for her, which I was happy to do. She was very pleased with my work.

One Saturday Hein asked me to sit on the frame of his bicycle and he would ride me back to his parents' farm. It was strictly forbidden for Adventists to do any kind of work on the Sabbath. One could do so only in case of extreme emergency, for instance to save one's life. This meant that there was a reason I could no longer stay with them. I did not ask any questions. We took off on the bicycle in the middle of the day in front of everyone.

"It is less dangerous this way," Hein explained.

I was dressed in a simple peasant girl's dress, a white kerchief on my head.

About two kilometers down the road, Hein turned off the highway and on to a farm road for about seven kilometers. He explained that he did this to avoid the German guards near the projectors, who stopped everybody to check documents.

Suddenly Hein started driving his bicycle as fast as he could, applying all his strength to the pedals. I did not understand what was happening at first. Only later I noticed a lot of German uniforms around.

"Look, there is a roundup search in this village. The farms are surrounded and the police are searching the houses." Hein was whispering to me. "Sit still. We cannot turn around; we've already been noticed. We'll try not to show fear and we may make it. We don't belong to this village."

We were both frightened and rode on, looking straight ahead. The police had not stopped us, taking us for natives and seeing that we rode in on them without fear. We left the police behind and reached the Viliumsons scared and out of breath. We were shaken by our encounter and knelt in a longer prayer to the Almighty for still another miracle.

"This is God's miracle," the old Viliumson said gravely. "He sees all and He guards us from evil. The benevolent sign of God is upon us. Hallelujah. Amen."

The faith of these people was strong. A faith in goodness, self-sacrifice without compromise, and they followed it in the face of great odds.

Hein left the same day, I remained with the Viliumsons but stayed hidden in the forest most of the time. Occasionally I would appear and work in the fields, then for a short time in the house, and again out of sight.

Another autumn was drawing near. The bloody war was already in its third year. How long can it go on? Is there an end?

I began to worry about the coming winter, the hardest time of year. My friend, Olivia, my trustworthy protector and defender, rode her bicycle to Riga to talk to the Kleibaises and ask if they would take me in for a while. They would. After a few days I walked to the city. Sasha and Greta took me in like a member

176

of the family. I was already familiar with their apartment and fit into their house routine. As before, I occupied myself with the household chores and sewing.

The Kleibaises rented out a room to two elderly sisters, Eichenberg. They too were Adventists and their relations with me were very friendly. Sasha and Greta introduced me to them as a Latvian friend from a farm village.

The old sisters took a liking to me and invited me to go to their church in the city. Sasha and Greta interceded and explained that I was of the same sect as the Viliumsons, whose rites were different from those of the old ladies. They grumbled a bit but did not press the point further. The relations remained friendly. For my part, I never left the house and kept myself busy inside.

The old man Kleibais, seeing how well I managed the house, decided that I would suit him for a wife. He started dressing in better clothes and handing out compliments and following me around the house. I was trying to avoid him and not listen to his invitations to marriage. I was countering that I had no right to get married because of my bad health. Being under the influence of liquor as usual, this argument did not satisfy him.

Of course, everyone in the house was aware of the situation. Sasha said once, half joking, half serious, "You know that my father is in love with you. This would be something if you were to marry him — you would be my mother," and she laughed.

"What are you saying, I am more suited to be his daughter than his wife," I replied. I did not care much for this trend in the conversation but it was repeated just about every day.

I stayed six weeks. It was time to leave.

10. *Frau Scheink Again*

Olivia always came up with another place for me to stay. This time she went to Frau Scheink and told her how good I was designing and making clothes; what wonderful dresses I made from old Jewish clothes for her sister-in-law and her sister-in-law's mother. It so happened that Frau Scheink's wardrobe was full of materials and clothes that needed remaking. Olivia praised my work so much that Frau Scheink actually begged her to bring me to her as soon as possible. Of course, to take me in was a great risk (but I could be of such great benefit), Herr Scheink might not like the idea (but how could he override his wife's whimsy?).

On the appointed day I walked to the Scheinks. Frau Scheink took me to the kitchen and repeated the old agreement, "If my husband likes you, then you can stay with us for a long time, and nobody will know."

To start with she gave me a whole mountain of clothes and linen to wash. I started immediately. The orderly for the German officer I had worked for in the beginning of the occupation had taught me a method of laundering I hadn't forgotten: not rubbing the clothes like most people do, but soaking them in a bathtub, then boiling them on the stove in a large kettle. This was faster and easier. Frau Scheink was skeptical at first of my methods, but on seeing the results, she agreed with me.

Noting that the laundering did not require much effort, Frau Scheink said, "You know, Anna, it is not really worthwhile to keep you washing clothes. I can do it myself. You had better start sewing."

"Whatever you say, Frau Scheink."

"I think we should start making a suit for my husband. That will please him very much."

"I don't know if I can do it. I have never made anything fancy for men. My specialty is women's clothes designing. What if I spoil some good material?"

"Try not to and I am sure you won't. Come, I'll show you a piece of alpaca that I have."

I was not in a position to argue. Tailoring work was like learning a new profession. Every stitch had to be done twice, also I had to redo a few steps. I worked fourteen to sixteen hours a day for three weeks. Finally came the time to try on the garment for a fit. I asked Mrs. Scheink to be present at the fitting, to be my consultant. Mainly I asked her to do this so she would not think there was something going on between me and her husband. She was a very suspicious wife when it came to her husband. Her jealousy bordered on obsession.

In the end my long and hard labors were crowned with success. Frau as well as Herr Scheink were so pleased with the garment that they decided to keep it as a dress-up suit.

After the suit, without pause, came Frau Scheink's clothes to be made. The first thing was an evening gown. She was in such ecstasy over it when it was finished that she immediately ran off to show it to her German neighbors.

The SS officers wanted to surprise their wives with finery, too, and were begging Frau Scheink to introduce them to such a fine master dressmaker. I don't know how she extricated herself from this predicament. She informed me that she told them her dressmaker was ill at this time, but she would introduce her to them as soon as she was better. Perhaps because of this incident Herr Scheink suggested to me the next day that he would try to get me some kind of documents to legalize my existence.

I listened. These were words, only words, no more. One needed friends "higher up" and money for a large bribe to obtain documents. Besides, it was very dangerous. Herr Scheink was not the man to take risks or be out a large sum of money, for a Jewess at that.

Frau Scheink, on the other hand, suggested that I brighten my hair with peroxide. She brought some peroxide and after a complicated procedure the job was done. I did not recognize myself when I looked in the mirror. Blond hair with brown eyes and a dark skin — quite a combination. Frau Scheink was quite satisfied with the results. She said that I now had an "Aryan" look. She asked me quite seriously: "Tell me, Anna, where do you come from by birth? Who were your ancestors. Your facial features indicate that you came from an aristocratic line."

"I am sorry to disappoint you, Frau Scheink, but my parents and their parents, as far as I know, were very ordinary people."

"No, my dear, I can recognize an aristocratic face when I see one. I am a specialist in the science of race purity."

From this time on her jealousy took on sickening aspects. She herself told me and was dropping hints that she was putting out traps by which I could be traced and caught doing a misdeed, such traps as gluing a small piece of paper across the door to see if I left the house to meet her husband while she was asleep.

I did go out late at night to catch some fresh air.

She always heard when I left and when I returned. Even though her husband was at her side, still she would interrogate me about whether I had designs on her husband or was secretly in love with him. I wanted to leave many a time, but where could I go in the middle of winter?

One day a surprise search of the apartment was carried out. It must have been that the SS men upstairs had become suspicious of Frau Scheink's finery that she boasted and her tangled stories about how she had acquired them.

When the knock on the door came I was eating hot cereal. Like a shot I was out of the kitchen, into a bedroom, squeezing myself under the eiderdown of the bed, careful not to disturb the outer appearance. I could hear a man's voice speaking politely to Frau Scheink. The bedroom door opened and the room was looked over superficially. The German officer was telling Frau Scheink something about the difficulties in billeting all the officers, about the necessity of sacrificing some comforts for the sake of victory, etc.

While they were standing right by the bed where I was hiding, I felt that my heart would fail from fear; my stomach was seized by terrible pains; the last mouthful of cereal was choking me. I was glad when Frau Scheink took the officer to examine the other rooms.

Later Herr Scheink found out that this check had indeed been made because of the garrulous boasting of Frau Scheink. The search, however, was a superficial one under the pretext of looking for temporary housing for officers. It was a good thing that Herr Scheink was on very good terms with his neighbors, otherwise they would have searched in a different manner.

I wanted to leave right away. Frau Scheink, however, would not have it; she insisted that I finish her dresses. As an afterthought she also decided that the apartment should have a general cleaning. For two days I scrubbed the walls, then stood on a stepladder and did the same to the smoke-tarnished ceiling. The apartment hadn't seen such a cleaning in years.

Frau Scheink followed me around directing and sighing once in a while, "Who will do the housecleaning, the sewing, the washing? It will be a great burden on me when you are gone."

I washed with soap and soda all ceilings, walls, and floors. The apartment sparkled with cleanliness and comfort. In turn, I looked like a chimneysweep. The dust and dirt, accumulated for years, ran down my head, my face, even over my back. I worked as hard as I could to carry out all her capricious orders.

"This is for the last time," she kept on saying. And for free, too, I added under my breath.

Herr Scheink also was well satisfied — and why not? He had never seen the house so clean and orderly, and no money out of his pocket for it.

There was one more debt to pay — the finishing of the dresses for Frau Scheink. I continued working hard to get them finished as quickly as possible. The Scheinks had relaxed by now and were trying to talk me into staying.

Herr Scheink said, "The worst is over. There are going to be no more searches. I fixed it all up."

I stayed. Where could I go? To the Viliumsons? I had stayed there long enough. Besides in winter there the food is scarce and there is no place to hide. So passed day after dreary day. Frau Scheink continued her fits of jealousy and never missed a chance to test my honesty.

When I was making up the beds one morning I found some candy scattered on the floor under the bed. I picked the pieces up and put them in a dish on the night table. I thought nothing about it until later in the day when Frau Scheink said, "You don't like candy?"

"I would rather have an extra piece of bread or a potato or cereal than candy," I replied.

Then it dawned on me: the scattered pieces of candy had been counted and put there as a trap. She was resorting to different tricks to test me so that it became a sort of game. My ration was not abundant; I could not eat as much or what I wanted. Food was doled out to me. There was many a time I went to bed half hungry. Thus I was warned always to be on guard because I could remain there only as long as I satisfied every whim of my benefactors.

Since the day of the search I had developed stomach pains. They were getting worse with every passing day. It got so bad I could not get up and keep food down. As though this wasn't enough, a boil on my back burst. I tried easing my pains with a hot water bottle. This is how it will end up at the Scheinks, I thought.

Frau Scheink said that she had had some medical training in a hospital and that she would take care of my boil. She took one look at it and lost her food. Sick as I was, I had to clean it up. It turned out that she knew as much about medicine as I did.

Things looked very grim. I could look for help from no one. On top of this Frau Scheink was complaining that the housework was not being done. She was also angry with me for washing the rags I used for bandages. She was deathly afraid of catching the infection. I thought at times I was on the brink of death with no medical aid or medicines, and my condition weakened by lack of food. I fought on, trying to hold myself together. Another miracle took place — I started improving and was soon well again. Somebody up there is looking out for me, I thought.

Frau Scheink was very happy, too: "I was so afraid for you when you were sick. If your boil had not opened, the pus would have gone inside your body and poisoned your whole system. You would surely have died. What would have happened to us then? How could we have gotten rid of your body? Thank God you are well again, thank God. The Lord is benevolent." And she went to pray.

As I regained my health, I resumed my chores as maid of all work. The Scheinks were never at a loss to find new work. So passed another winter. The cold was gone, the trees were budding, green grass sprouted here and there.

The Scheinks decided to make a vegetable garden in their back yard and, of course, I was to do the work. I was terrified of going outside in the daylight. "The officers will see me."

"Don't be frightened," Frau Scheink assured me, "this will not be dangerous. I will tell them that I hired a woman to work for me."

I started digging up the ground, always trying to keep my back to the house. I was also wearing a dark head kerchief to shield my face as much as possible. The officers did ask Frau Scheink who that bent woman was, working away all day in the yard. They believed her explanation and paid no more attention to me.

On occasion, when Frau Scheink felt well disposed toward me, she would philosophize, "You know,

Anna, sometimes I wonder how you can carry on like this for years, all by yourself, without medical help, and still stay alive."

"You believe in God just as I do. Life is God's will, His miracle. He gives life to whom He wants, in the face of all obstacles."

"Yes, yes, you are right, it is all from God. You know, the Germans are carting away whole groups of Jews, even now, to be shot in the forests."

I felt faint and turned pale. She continued, "That father and son whom I wanted to place at Pesla's — they too are not among the living . . . They offered me quite a lot of jewelry, gold, diamonds, rubies . . . It is a shame that I couldn't do a thing for them . . . I don't even know where they were killed."

Herr Scheink used to turn on the radio in the evening to listen to the news. It happened that I was clearing the table after dinner at the time and listened intently. It was a London broadcast in German. The fortunes of the Germans were bad on all fronts. The Reds were attacking in the Ukraine and in White Russia; the English were pushing Rommel around in Africa; the partisans were hitting them in the rear. I was playing dumb as though I hadn't heard or understood a thing. Inside, I was jubilant — soon, soon there will be salvation. Will I make it?

"What do you think, Anna," Frau Scheink interrupted my thoughts. "My husband wants me to go to the movies. Shall I go?"

"If the picture is good, why shouldn't you go?" I answered, forgetting the Adventist taboo on entertainment.

"But this is forbidden for us faithful. It is a sin to go to the theater, the cinema, the opera." She was obviously fighting with her conscience and at the same time testing me. I felt this right away. I was caught and was trying to smooth it over.

I said, "A little sin sometimes might be allowed in certain circumstances. It really wouldn't look good to let your husband go by himself."

"I will take your advice."

They did go. I was to blame for her sin. From here on her regard for me was very low indeed. Now she was sure that if I could advise her to sin before God, then I could and probably had been sinning with her husband.

"I feel it, I know it," she tormented me, "there is something going on between you two."

"How can you say such things? I am a sick girl, ugly, unkempt, thin as a skeleton. Do you think your husband would prefer me to such a beautiful well-built and devoted wife?"

"I don't know. I hope for my sake and yours that what you say is true. I still have a feeling that something is not quite right. I have a good intuition and a good sense of smell. It is the way you look at him, sideways, the way you avoid talking to him in my presence, the way you never look him straight in the eye when he talks to you. You must have a guilty conscience. Oh, may God strike you down if you are lying to me. Why did I ever get tied up with you?"

"May God strike me down if I lied to you. May God forgive you for the false accusations."

Suddenly there was a loud knock on the door. I only had time to run into the bedroom and hide behind the open door. Two SS men were there. They talked politely to Frau Scheink, I could not make out about what. Then they leisurely walked through every room in the house. One went into the bedroom where I was hiding, had a quick look around and left. I heard them apologizing for the disturbance and close the door.

We were shaken by their sudden visit. It was the last straw for all of us. "Anna must leave immediately," Herr Scheink said to his wife. "I will not have my life endangered over this Jewess, even if she is of your faith."

That was that. I was really glad. They were finally willing to let me go before thinking of more things for me to "finish."

Frau Scheink gave me a couple of old dresses and a woolen shawl to wrap up in. In parting, she said, "Could be you will be saved and you will stay alive."

"If God wants me to live, then so it will be," I replied.

"Most likely we will have to run . . . leave everything . . . ours are not doing so well on the fronts."

She looked confused and pitiful. I had never seen her like this. A few days previously I had noticed both of them digging in the back yard. When they came into the house Herr Scheink was carrying a round metal box. This was the first sign of "suitcase fever." It probably contained their accumulated wealth which did not take much space or weigh much, and was legal tender wherever they might go — gold, coins, diamonds, jewels.

"You go now and give my greetings to Olivia. Don't come back here, ever, no matter what." Frau Scheink was really aroused. "I know there was something between you and my husband regardless of what you say. You ate my bread and stayed under my roof, and you paid me back with . . ."

She was hissing. I ran out of the door and into the street, turned around for a glance at where I had spent the hard winter. Frau Scheink was at the window, eyes flashing hate and reproach.

You fool, I wished I could say to her. Your husband held no interest for me. When you start running, when all your thoughts and energies are consumed with how to get a piece of bread, or where to stay overnight, when your life hangs by a thread, then maybe you will understand.

Off to Katlakalns, to my only friends left in this world, the wonderful Viliumsons.

11. The Final Ordeals

The years of wandering and the experience of living one day at a time gave me a confidence that I could not have had before, a confidence that somehow I would survive, that Someone was watching over me, that I had a mission to perform. But with the confidence a certain amount of carelessness crept in.

I decided to take the streetcar to the other side of the Dvina River close to the Bauskas Highway. I would not have dared to do that a year ago. Lowering my head, I mixed in the group of people and went inside the car. No sooner had I occupied my seat than I felt I was being examined by many suspicious eyes. One lady passenger especially would not take her eyes off me. I had to do something fast and resorted to my old trick that had worked before — talk in my best Latvian and look unconcerned.

"The car is not crowded today," I remarked to my neighboring passenger. "The other day I took the same car and nearly got squeezed to death. Couldn't even reach the string for the bell, had to shout to the conductor to stop."

"It is hard to predict with this car. When one is crowded, I wait for the next car and it is empty, so one can even stretch out and go to sleep."

"I had the same experience."

"I went to the city for some flower seeds and there is a shortage even of these. I usually make a little extra money selling flowers in the fall. I'll have to do with what I've got."

"I plant all in vegetables that you can eat and sell, too."

The atmosphere gradually relaxed and people stopped paying attention to me. There was the end of the line with the circle to turn the car around. I had another twenty kilometers to walk.

I was weak and my back hurt. The furuncle was now an open wound; my stomach ached and my feet were barely moving as I threaded my way bent like an old woman and this time I did not have to fake it. The road seemed endless. By evening I was nearing the Viliumson farm, making a detour of a few kilometers to avoid the Germans guarding the light projectors.

Everyone was frightened when I finally stumbled into the Viliumson house later that night. I had aged a great deal and must have looked bad. Olivia ran to me and embraced me when she saw who I was. A good meal, rest, and being surrounded by friends who really cared did wonders for me.

I had to tell them how I had fared through the winter at the Scheinks and could leave out no details. They were eager for news. When I told them about Frau Scheink's jealous tantrums, Olivia burst out laughing.

"Frau Scheink is crazy. Jealousy of her husband is her obsession. She was even jealous of her own mother. She suspected her of having secret meetings with her husband. She is afraid of her husband, though. She won't tell him a thing."

After my story, Mr Viliumson started bringing me up to date on conditions on the farm. "The situation here is much different than when you left. Quite often we have unexpected searches and everyone must show documents. Their searches now are thorough; they have more experience, I guess. Sometimes they come in large numbers and surround a place so that nobody can escape. Your safest place to stay will be the forest. Even there you will have to be on constant watch because they search there too sometimes. We'll help you all we can with food."

"I am very grateful for your kindness and concern," I said. "I need the fresh air and sunshine that I have been deprived of for so long. It is warm enough now even at night. I will enjoy living there."

"Would you like me to come and stay with you sometimes for company?" Olivia asked.

"Not now, dear," I said. "The ground is still too damp and the air is moist and chilly at night. It wouldn't do for your cough. Pretty soon when we start mowing hay, then we'll enjoy each other's company."

Mrs. Viliumson gave me a blanket and off I went into the night. It took me a while until I got used to the darkness in the moonless night. Gradually I started discerning outlines off the path, a tree here, a bush there. I settled on the bushes. One could hide easily, not be seen but could see out. I wrapped myself in the blanket, curled up on the still damp grass and fell asleep almost immediately — what bliss!

My strength returned with every passing day. The sun, the fresh air, the simple nutritious peasant food were my best medicine. When hay making time came I was fit and eager to go to work.

With a clear sky for cover, standing there in a green sea of grass gently waving in the breeze, wielding the long handle of the scythe was a pleasure hard to describe. One has to experience the feel of his strength, his power in cutting the grass. Swish — cut — step forward; swish — cut — step forward, and so on until one had cut a swath through the meadow. The grass was left on the ground to dry in the sun. The next row was started and so on until the meadow was bare with only stubble showing. The fresh cut smell of hay was overwhelming and invigorating. After the hay had dried, we piled it in conical haystacks. When the meadow belonging to the Viliumsons was finished, Mr. Viliumson took me through the forest about twenty-five kilometers to another string of little meadows. He had received special permission to mow hay there for free. He showed me the place and rode back home, leaving me by myself. I liked it that way very much — the farther away from people, the better.

For many kilometers around me there was no sign of man — only trees, birds singing, the occasional grunt of an animal. I felt free, free of the fear that had been haunting me for such a long time, that had been gnawing my insides. I started working with great relish. Near evening I had two haystacks made and more hay drying. The air had become sultry and high clouds appeared in the sky. A thunderstorm was brewing. I made myself a bed on the bottom of one haystack and crawled in. I was nibbling on my food as the first lightning flashed, followed by reverberations of thunder. The sun was blanked out by swiftly moving clouds and a wind started blowing, first gently, then increasing in intensity. I could see the trees swaying and hear the plop, plop of the first raindrops. The rain came down harder and harder. It seemed that the lightning was flashing incessantly and there was no letup to the thunder. God is speaking angrily, I thought, which was something my mother used to say long, long ago. My haystack was inundated pretty soon and I was soaked through. It was good that the night was warm and I rather enjoyed the display of nature's fury. The rain stopped as suddenly as it had started. Stars appeared in the sky and amused me through the sleepless night.

The sun came out early at this time of year. It promised to be a hot day. I scattered the two haystacks to dry. I found six snakes in one and killed them all with my scythe.

A few days later old Mr. Viliumson came riding in with a huge hay wagon. We both packed a load and I rode home with him. There we unloaded the hay into a stack and made a roof over it to protect it from rain. I made a hole inside it to spend the night. I slept well but had a nightmare. I felt a black snake around my throat ready to strike. I wanted to cry out but couldn't. Then by a miracle the snake loosened its coils and went away. I woke up soaked with perspiration. I was not so sure that it was a nightmare; it may have really happened. I still shudder when I think of it.

After the haying came the berries and mushrooms. Olivia and I went often into the forest to gather the bounty, enough for ourselves and to sell in the city. Olivia was careful always to have matches with her. She said, "Never go into the forest without matches from now on. I was told that big wolf packs were roaming our forests now. The war front had driven them close to us. I heard they attacked a woman carrying a baby. Only some peasants who happened along rescued the woman, but the baby was chewed up. Wolves are afraid of fire. At the first sign of wolves, when they howl, make a fire and they won't come near you."

Day after day we would bring back full, heavy baskets of berries and mushrooms. I started carrying matches and listened to every little noise at night that might signal an approaching wolf pack. When one lives a long time in the forest he becomes a part of it. I could recognize every little noise whether it was a rat or a squirrel scampering around, a fox chasing a young deer, the screech of a bat, the hoot of an owl. I was aware of what was going on around me even when I was asleep. The story of the wolves did not disturb my sleep for my ears were listening for them.

Good news started seeping back to us in the village. The Germans were not doing so well. The Red Army took Yelgava which was very close to us. A wave of happy excitement took hold of me. My mind started making plans how to cross the front lines.

A few days later some neighbors were discussing the war at the Viliumson house. "I heard that ours took Yelgava back from the Reds."

"Not only did they take Yelgava but they pushed them back about 150 kilometers."

"With heavy losses."

"Ours launched a counteroffensive."

"I think it is more a straightening of the lines, stabilizing the front, than a major counteroffensive."

"Don't discount our forces; they have plenty of strength left. We had reverses before but we came out on top in the end."

I don't know what happened to me; it could be the news that Yelgava was retaken by the Germans, but I burst out in a rage, "Hitler is finished, don't you see? He was at the gates of Moscow and Stalingrad, and now he is only 100 kilometers from here. He lost an army, not just a division, at Stalingrad. He is running out of food, out of ammunition, and out of men. He is scraping the barrel."

Olivia did not let me finish. The neighbors were visibly shaken by my daring speech. Looking at me with reproach, she said, "It is God's will. It will be the way He orders it. It is shameful for us to discuss war and especially to argue about it."

Everyone, especially I, felt embarrassed. The

neighbors left, one by one, and Olivia and I were left by ourselves. I burst into tears. She put her arms around me, consoling me in her tender voice, "There, there, have a good cry. I know you did not mean to put us in jeopardy. You just couldn't hold back. I only hope it does not get back to the authorities."

"I hope so, too," I sobbed. "I don't know what came over me. I am very sorry. I hope you will not suffer because of it."

* * *

The summer was coming to an end; August was nearly gone. The Reds were clearing Latvia but Riga was still held by the Germans. Olivia went to Riga with berries and mushrooms for her friends. She returned with breathtaking news — the Germans were preparing to surrender Riga. Before they did that, however, they were robbing the city of its treasures and sending them back to Germany. On top of that they were taking all the men in the army, even the ones who had been excused for one reason or another, and driving them back to Germany.

The total mobilization hit the Viliumsons as well. The Germans had taken Hein, even though he was a conscientious objector. It is forbidden for Adventists to carry arms. The Germans, however, did assign him to be a cook in one of the military divisions in Latvia. This at least saved him from the front lines.

During one of these early sunny autumn days, it was fate again to walk the tightrope of life over the precipice to death. It happened in the middle of September on a Saturday afternoon.

I came home to the Viliumson house after a week's stay in the forest. I used to do this to clean up, change my clothes, and replenish my food supply. I lay down in my clothes on the bed to rest after the long walk.

195

Suddenly a car raced up to the house. Three drunken Germans and one Latvian jumped out of the car and without a knock pushed themselves into the house. I was trapped.

"Who lives here?" the Latvian asked in businesslike tones.

"My wife, my daughter, and a woman who comes to help us with the garden chores," Mr. Viliumson answered, visibly shaken.

"Please bring your house book," the Latvian continued.

Everybody was scared. Old Mrs. Viliumson felt faint and sat down on her bed. Mr. Viliumson was digging into all kinds of papers to find his house book. The Germans were looking around the house and making fun of things. Mr. Viliumson finally found the house book and handed it to the Latvian, his hands shaking. The Latvian looked through the book, then pointed a finger to me and asked, "Who is this woman?"

I stayed with my face down in the pillow and did not move, thinking only how fate could play such tricks. To escape death so many times, and when liberation is so near (the Reds were only twenty to thirty kilometers from here), to get caught in such a stupid way.

"She is an acquaintance of ours," Ferdinand Viliumson answered in a shaky voice. "She helps us with our garden chores, as I have explained."

I broke out in a cold sweat.

"Then why is she not registered in your book?" one of the Germans shouted the question.

"She only came here yesterday and today is Saturday, our Sabbath, so there was no time to go to the city hall and register her," Mr. Viliumson lamely tried to find an excuse.

I still kept down. A hurricane raged within me, like it had in the Rumbuli forest during the shootings. I already could see myself being dragged outside and shot in the yard for all to see. The Viliumsons would suffer the same fate. The house would be burned to the ground; they would slaughter the whole village.

One of the Germans came to my bed, nudged me, and shouted, "Who are you? Show your documents!"

As though I'd been scalded with hot water, I jumped off the bed. Covering my face with my hands, I started screaming shrilly in Latvian, "What do you want of me? I don't understand German. Shoot me, go ahead and shoot me!"

I collapsed on my knees, my head touching the floor, and started sobbing loudly and unceasingly.

Everybody was taken aback, startled with my performance. The Latvian regained his composure and in a soft manner translated the German's request: "We want to see your documents, show us your documents."

I jumped up in a flash and screamed, "Documents! Documents they want! I barely escaped with my life from those damned, a thousand times damned, bolsheviks. They killed my husband, my children, burned . . ."

"Where did you run from?" the Latvian persisted.

"From Gulbene. They burned our house and barns, drove off our livestock, killed the chickens. Ruined. Everything is in ruins. I am the only one who escaped. I was picking berries in the forest when they came. Somebody denounced us as Nazi adherents. They were shooting at me when I was crossing the lines . . . and you want documents. All I have is the clothes on my back."

I went on sobbing again, covering my face. There was quiet for a few moments. One of the Germans came by and nudged me again, "Sprechen sie Deutsch?"

"Nikt shpreken," I mumbled, not looking at him.

"Tell her to go tomorrow and register with the refugees and she will be sent to Germany," the German was telling the Latvian in German and the latter translated to me in Latvian. I nodded my heat in assent.

They returned the house book to Mr Viliumson, clicked their heels, saluted, and departed with a roar of their automobile.

We stood there a long time as if rooted to the spot, not believing our eyes and ears, as though it had not happened.

Finally, Mr. Viliumson came and embraced me and kissed me on the forehead, and with tears in his eyes said, "I was sure we were going to see our Maker. Glory to the Almighty. His powerful hand was here to save us all."

We all fell to our knees and prayed for a long, long time.

With the first light the next morning, Mrs. Urkevich, our neighbor, came running over. As soon as she closed the door and without greetings, she started her story breathlessly: "After the policemen visited your house, they came to us. They sat my father-in-law in a chair, surrounded him, and started interrogating him. They were trying to get information from him about deserters, about your family, about Anna. They tried all kinds of tricks on him; they threatened to shoot him; they pulled on his beard, but the old man was steadfast in saying that he knew nothing about deserters, knew nothing bad about the Viliumsons and had never heard of Anna. After an hour of mocking, threatening, and taunting the old man, they let him go. Before they left, they shouted that they would shoot and burn up the whole village if they found that anyone had lied."

"Times are bad and getting worse," Mr. Viliumson said.

Later that afternoon the two Germans that had visited the day before came by to remind Mr. Viliumson not to procrastinate and to send me away to registration and evacuation. This happened while I was working in the garden in front of the house. As usual I looked away so as not to betray my black forbidden eyes.

They entered the house and repeated the same to the landlords.

When the Germans had gone and were out of sight, Mr. Viliumson came out and told me what had transpired. "You must leave, Anna, the sooner the better. If not, we all might perish."

"I understand," I said.

I packed a few clothes and some food in my basket. The parting was sad. I was on my way again.

I cut across the field and into the forest, avoiding traveled paths and roads. My plans were to make it across the main highway to Riga and to get to the shore of the Dvina River. There I might be able to hitch a ride on a boat down the river and lose myself in the city. As I neared the highway I was careful to look in all directions and waited for a time when all traffic was clear before attempting to cross.

I saw a woman on a bicycle approaching. It was Olivia. She was coming from the city. Forgetting all precautions, I ran out of the forest to intercept her.

She stopped, and seeing me dressed for a trip, she shouted, "Where are you going? Are you crazy or something? The Germans are thicker than fleas in summertime. Let's get away from here."

We turned into the forest. I told her everything that had happened and that there was no way but to leave and not subject the best and only friends I had left in the world to mortal danger.

"And where do you think you can go now?"

"I really don't know; perhaps Sasha and Greta could take me in."

"You are out of your mind. Riga is the one place you shouldn't go to. There is panic and chaos. The Germans are nervous and scared by Red saboteurs and spies. You couldn't make it for two blocks without having your documents checked. Woe to the one who doesn't have them with him; they shoot him right then and there. No, you'll never make it to Sasha's."

"Then where can I go?"

"You know what? I have a plan. Let us ask God. If He says yes, then go to the city; if He says no, then you go back to the village."

"How are you going to ask Him and do you think we will be able to understand His advice?"

"You'll see in just a minute. Let's walk along the highway."

She pulled me after her. To think, she is going to speak to God Himself; she must be out of her mind, I was thinking.

"Look, here I have two pieces of paper. I marked one and the other is blank. Now I am going to roll them into little tubes and throw them on the road." She did as she said, then picked up the little paper tubes and exclaimed, "Aha, you see, this one pointing toward the forest and the other toward Riga. Now, the marked one is pointing to the forest. That means that God wills you to go back."

There was a shine to her eyes as though she was putting something over on me. I did not care to argue and was glad at the turn of events.

"But where should I go?"

"Into the forest. You've lived there before. This is the least dangerous place and you don't involve anybody else."

We started back at a fast pace. I kept thinking about Olivia — a simple peasant girl with so much feeling for her fellow man, so much sensitivity and wise beyond her years. She had pulled me out of tight spots so many times that I began to believe she was my guardian angel.

Short of the Viliumson house, Olivia said, "Wait for me at the edge of the forest. I'll be back quickly. I have something for you."

When she came back she triumphantly held up the little spade we had found one day in the forest. "It may come in handy where you are going; it can do many things; you can defend yourself with it. And here are some matches, too. Remember what I told you. Now go before dark sets in. The raspberry bramble has a hole in it like a cave and would make a comfortable hiding place. I'll meet you there tomorrow."

We parted with embraces. I knew where the raspberry bramble was. Many times Olivia and I had picked berries there. It was about three kilometers' walk and I reached it as darkness fell. I did not dare go farther in the darkness because just beyond it was swampy cranberry country.

The night was damp and cold even though it was only September. I sat with my back against an old pine tree and did not dare move. I listened to every little noise, clutching the little spade and the matches, my only weapons against wolves. The dampness was penetrating, and the cold with it.

As soon as it got light enough so I could look around, I started walking back and forth, back and forth, to loosen up my joints and get the blood flowing again. Then I started looking for a good place to make a hideout home. I chose a hillock on top of which stood a tall pine tree. All around it grew raspberry bushes. I started digging a hole with my rusty little spade. The roots of the tree were interwoven with the roots of neighboring trees and they were not far from the surface. I dug underneath the roots so that my hole was actually below them. I cleaned out the dirt between the roots and climbed in for a trial — it looked good. I could not quite stretch out full length, but it offered shelter and was completely hidden.

Olivia came to visit me in the afternoon. She found my dugout excellent and tried it out herself. She said it was completely invisible from the outside. She stayed with me until evening and told me that the German police came to their house again to verify that I had left for Riga and registration. She promised to visit me often and bring food.

The second night I spent in my "own new home." It wasn't very roomy when I had all my warm clothes on. Each time I made a small motion sand would start falling from above on my face. The same thing happened when the wind swayed the tree. I lay there but could not sleep. One thought haunted me; this will be my grave, a grave that I have dug for myself. Here I will meet the end. It gave me an eerie, weird feeling.

From the depths of the forest I heard animal

sounds and bird calls once in a while. This did not bother me; I was used to them. It was the noises of human footsteps that I was listening for in fright.

The next day I increased the size of my lair, then took away the dirt I had dug out and dispersed it far away. Tall dry sedge grasses placed on the bottom of the hole made me a more comfortable bed.

One day I went out on my daily foraging expedition for berries and mushrooms. When I returned to my hole I found a fox comfortably spread out in my dugout. I was not going to give up my lair to an intruder. I lifted my spade threateningly and hissed at him. Just as threateningly he bared his teeth and growled. I made a step forward and hit the tree root with the spade. He knew I meant business then, and out he went, his bushy tail waving, and disappeared into the forest.

This made me think that now I am an animal; I'll live like one and fight for what is mine.

The days were dragging on uneventfully. Olivia did not come to visit. This worried me very much. Maybe the Germans had driven them to Germany or mobilized them in forced labor groups. Serious things must have happened to prevent her from coming. I had too much time to think and worry.

It was about a week or so after I had established myself as the "queen of the forest" when I heard voices, human voices. I listened carefully and distinguished German speech. This hit me hard — the Germans are here, too. Where else can I go now?

I stayed in my hole, not daring to go out, and used my time to camouflage myself with dry twigs and sod I pulled from the rim of my dugout.

Noises of wood sawing, an ax chopping and trees falling could be heard distinctly. The Germans must be building some kind of fortification. Then the front must be near! The hammering of nails, the talk, the laughter died down with the coming of evening. They did not dare light fires. Everything was quiet for the night.

With the first rays of light I left my hiding place and crawled behind the raspberry bushes, then lost myself deeper in the forest. I started picking mushrooms and was absorbed in my work. Suddenly a a group of military boots appeared in front of me. One glance told me they were Latvians in German uniform. I kept in a bent position.

"What are you doing here?" one of the group asked.

"I am gathering mushrooms," I answered, not raising my head. Blood gushed out of my nose from excitement and fright. I covered my face with a kerchief and squeezed my nose to stop the bleeding.

"How do we find the road out?" another asked.

"There," I pointed, "take this direction and a few kilometers farther you will come to the Riga highway."

They left. Hours later, I was still shaking from fright. It was dangerous to go to my hideout during the day so I wandered all over the forest. When evening came I crawled quietly back to my hole. I could see in the twilight some kind of structures that the Germans had erected. They must have been planning to stay here for a long time.

* * *

Two weeks passed and Olivia did not appear. I was sure now that something horrible had happened to the Viliumsons. My food was long gone. I was now on a ration of berries and mushrooms — this still left me hungry. The worst, however, was thirst. The berries did not satisfy my thirst or hunger either. I went deeper into the forest where there used to be swampland with puddles of water, but they were dry now. My lips were dry and parched. I started digging with my little spade but no water came.

One day a terrific shelling started up suddenly when I was out in the open. Bombs whistled through the air and exploded in the distance; then the bombing came a little closer. I could see some trees being hit. Now the Reds had found out that Germans were up here. I was elated, but it hurt to see the bombs hitting off target and being wasted. I was closer to being hit than the Germans, but was glad just the same. They'll get to them, I told myself.

I started crawling up the hill to my hiding place. Again a whole volley of bombs started falling, this time from airplanes. The Germans were spotted! I almost jumped for joy. Now the Reds were hitting the target. The German structures were going up in flames; I could hear shouts and screams — the Germans were catching it.

I finally made it to my cave and climbed in. The cannonade and shooting continued on the rest of the day. Now between bomb and shell explosions I could hear machine gun and rifle fire — the front was right here!

I was so happy I could hardly contain myself staying in my cave. I wanted to jump and dance and shout, "Pour it on, pour it on! Let them have a taste of their own medicine!" But my thirst brought me back to reality. I had to force myself not to give in, not to lose my mind, not to faint.

What can I do? Liberation is so close. If God has kept me alive for so long, through so many perils, He will give me strength to overcome this, too. Thus I kept my spirits up. I even got used to the bombardment, the rat-ta-ta of the machine guns, the attacks and counterattacks. The more bombs are dropped, the more fire is poured on them, the closer my liberation comes.

Three weeks had passed since Olivia's last visit. I could wait no longer. It would be ironic to die of thirst. I decided to risk the chances and cut across the front. An idea struck me, the Viliumson farm may be liberated already, that is why Olivia could not come. It seemed very logical. So, early the next morning before daybreak, I set out for the Viliumson farm with a full basket of mushrooms.

With some misgivings I approached the German fortifications. I could see a lot of splintered wood and craters caused by the bombs. There were a few soldiers working around a camp stove. To my surprise, nobody stopped me. They must have taken me for a local farmer's wife out collecting mushrooms.

I dropped all precaution at the sight of a well near a farm and drew a bucket for myself. I drank and drank and drank. One has to experience weeks of thirst to really appreciate the taste of water. I read somewhere that after a prolonged time without water, one should not drink too much at one time. It was hard to tear myself away from that bucket.

At the Viliumson well I stopped and drank some more, this time all I could hold. I approached the Viliumson house cautiously, looking out at it from behind some bushes. Some strangers were walking around the yard. I also noticed several German cars, one wrecked, a field kitchen, several camouflaged cannon, and Germans talking.

I decided to wait until some of the family came out. After a while the old Mrs. Viliumson came out and went to the well. I came out to meet her. She was startled. "Where did you come from?"

"I have been in the forest since I left you."

"We thought that you went with the refugees to Germany. For God's sake, do not go in the house. They have made an army barracks of our house." She was in a panic.

"Don't be afraid, I only came for a drink of water and a little food if you can spare it, then I will leave."

Olivia came running out, tears of joy in her eyes. We embraced. Her mother left — it was dangerous to stay in a group. The Germans would be suspicious.

"I was so worried about you, Anna. Alone in the forest, without food and with all the shooting and bombardment. Thank God you are well. I tried several times to go see you but each time I was stopped by the military. They would not let anybody through because it was, they said, a war theater and too dangerous for civilians. You know how I felt about that?"

"I was worried about you, too, but afraid to come out. The Germans have built some bunkers and trenches near my hideout and I dare not go in or out except in the dark. Further on is the swamp and I am afraid to go there. What is going on here?"

"Chaos, in one word it is chaos. The Germans made it a military staff point. There is no room for you to hide. You will have to go back to the forest. Soldiers come and go — they sleep everywhere."

She disappeared into the house while I busied myself washing the mushrooms at the well. Olivia did not look well. She was pale and thin and hard dark circles under her eyes. Only her pleasant smile and that sparkle of goodness on her face were still there, but the cough and wheezing came with every breath. God help her.

Olivia came out with a big basket of food and two bottles filled with water. "Here, take this. This will take care of you for some time. Listen to me, don't try to cross the front. You'll be killed. Go back to the forest and hide in your hole. That is the safest place. Remember what I say — don't dare cross the front."

Again we parted with an embrace. I went back to the forest, making a big detour to avoid the German military watch. It would not be healthy to be caught and accused of spying, without documents, and a Jew . . .

I walked fast, chewing on bread and cheese to still my hunger. I hadn't had solid food for over two weeks.

I'll wander through the forest until dark and then stealthily crawl to my hole, I was thinking. Suddenly bombs started exploding all around me. The forest caught fire. Flames and clouds of smoke were billowing upwards and blocking my way. Luckily the wind was flowing toward the German fortifications and away from the direction whence I had come. The tree guarding my hideout was in the path of the fire. I stopped. To continue meant certain death, if not by fire and smoke, then by a bullet or bomb fragments. I lay down, hidden by bushes, and waited to see what would happen. The forest fire was slowing down. The small arms fire and the bomb explosions receded, then started again several times. There was nothing to do but go back, come what would.

I was slowly approaching the Viliumson farm and observing what was going on. Men, automobiles, motorcycles were coming and going. The yard was full of activity. Nobody paid any attention to me, but Olivia saw me and ran to meet me.

"I had to come back," I said, "the forest is on fire.

On top of that, there is a big fight going on with lots of shooting and bombardment."

"It's good you came back," Olivia had her arm around me. "The Germans just changed personnel. They are coming and going. You can stay with us now. We'll tell them that you are a neighbor. These are military men, not SS or police. They are less suspicious; besides, it looks as though they have their hands full and things are not going so well. They won't even notice you."

I did not risk going into the house, however. There were many staff officers and this type doesn't change much. Instead, I made myself a bed of straw in the stall next to the cow and the roosting chickens. In the evening, as Mrs. Viliumson came to milk the cow, an SS man came looking for deserters.

"Who is that woman?" he growled in German, pointing to me.

Mrs. Viliumsons started shaking. "She, she is our neighbor's daughter."

The German looked over the dung hill. His face grimaced. The stench had probably got to him. "Do not let strangers in here," and he walked away.

"Thanks to the Almighty," the old one mumbled. "Guard us from all intruders."

She was still shaking so badly that I had to finish the milking. We went out together in view of everyone and stood as though talking for a while, then she gave me a sign to rush back into the stall and she closed the door behind me. A click of the lock told me that I was locked in for the night.

The pile of manure was reaching up to the ceiling. The stench was getting unbearable. I felt I would die for lack of fresh air. It seemed that the cow too was breathing hard and gasping for air.

I ran to the little window but found it boarded over from the outside. I was getting light headed and felt faint. My God! Surely You haven't protected me for three years from all harm only to have me perish on a heap of dung. I prayed. And suddenly something flashed in my mind — the pitchfork! Somewhere I had seen a pitchfork. After a frantic search in the dark my hands felt the smooth, round handle leaning against the wall near the door. One swing of the handle against the window and the boards came loose with a cracking sound. I was so desperate that I didn't care if it woke up the whole German army, but no attention was paid to the noise.

I greedily sucked in the fresh night air and stood the rest of the night near the window. I considered squeezing myself through the opening but it was too small.

With the first morning light came a click of the lock. Old Mrs. Viliumson stood in the door. She came to milk the cow.

"I am so glad to see you," I hugged and kissed her, tears running down my face.

"What is it, Anna, why are you crying? You are trembling."

"I was almost suffocated last night after you locked the door. There wasn't enough air in here. The window was nailed shut. I am sorry but I had to break it open."

Mrs. Viliumson turned pale. "Mr. Viliumson had forgotten to open the window for the summer. He closes it to protect the cow from the winter cold. I always leave the door open and only locked it to protect you from being molested during the night. You could have been asphyxiated along with the cow and the chickens. I heard once that manure gives off noxious gases, especially when it gets warm. Oh, my child, I could never have forgiven myself if anything had happened to you. Olivia is right when she says that you are holy. God is protecting you. He has given you the wisdom and the tool to break out the window."

"I intended to climb out of the window and spend the night in the hay."

"Don't think of such a thing. There are six or more soldiers in every haystack. There are soldiers in every nook and cranny, even in the cellar. They stay overnight and leave, then others come for an overnight's stay."

I milked the cow and handed the pail to Mrs. Viliumson. She turned to me in the doorway, "Stay here until the soldiers leave. I'll talk to Olivia and see what we can come up with."

The noises increased as the day grew lighter. People were running back and forth; voices were giving commands. The smell of cooking wafted in. I could see through the window soldiers with messkits lined up before the field kitchen. More and more soldiers were coming to the kitchen from all directions. Some of them were leaving with steaming kettles.

Olivia appeared at the door. "Follow me quickly while the soldiers are milling around and the staff is busy with their morning orders." She led me into the unfinished room. "You will have to play sick for a few days, Anna. Take your clothes off, put on this nightshirt, and jump into bed."

Olivia put a stool at the bedside and placed medicine bottles and pill boxes on top of it. I sat up in bed and started knitting a sweater for Olivia.

The German officer staff was in the next room. I

could see through the window that traffic outside was heavy. Military people were coming in on motorcycles and bicycles about every minute. They would run into the house and after a few minutes out again, then others would come. Judging by their faces, the situation must be very grave.

The Germans were being pressed from all directions. They had a hard time trying to save their troops and weapons during the retreat.

Olivia was looking very pale. Her illness was in an advanced stage. Blood showed in her cough. She spent most of her time with me in bed, staring at the ceiling for hours, her blue eyes sad. Her breath came with pain and produced a wheezing sound. Her life was dimming before my eyes. My heart was tearing apart — here was my best friend in this world in great suffering and I helpless to do a thing for her. I tried to comfort and encourage her.

"It looks as though the war is coming to an end. Pretty soon I'll be able to go out in the open and I'll take you to a hospital in Riga and get a specialist to help you."

"My dear Anna, I know your heart is good, but I am afraid it is too late. I may not see another spring." Tears started slowly coursing down her face. She did not try to wipe them away. She knew.

Ruti came to see us. Kurt sent her, he was worried about us. He could not come himself, they would not let him leave his job — the Germans needed flour. She was to consult with us whether to stay or leave with the retreating Germans.

There was confusion in the area that bordered on panic. The Germans were retreating and it seemed that the front was right here. The air was full of thunderous noise from all kinds of weapons: a rapid staccato of machine guns, faraway thunder of big guns as though someone was beating on a big drum, then cra — a — ack, a shell would explode. Small arms fire could be heard during the intervals of the bigger noisemakers.

Interesting how people can get used to any situation. Life at the Viliumsons proceeded as routinely as ever. Only the military people seemed excited. Troops, in trucks and on foot, were passing by, occasionally halting for a hurried meal, faces drawn. Gone was the arrogance, the joking, the horseplay — they were beaten and they knew it, no matter if the official line called it "temporary setback," "front stabilization," "shortening of the lines of transportation" . . . They were beaten. I was jubilant — a few more days and the nightmare would be over.

Olivia decided to let Ruti in on my "secret," so that she would not unwittingly say something to the Germans that might give me away. She called her into our room and started talking to her in a whisper. I could see Ruti's face grow pale and droplets of sweat stand out on her forehead as the story progressed. She would lift frightened eyes at me from time to time in disbelief and bewilderment.

"God in heaven have mercy upon us and protect us," Ruti finally said, when Olivia finished her tale. We sat for some time in silence. Ruti was digesting what she had just learned.

She sighed and got up. Olivia pulled her down to the chair again and started talking fast, with her eyes flashing animatedly: "I knew you would understand. We saved a soul for God. You can help. The Germans are very suspicious and nervous now. Often SS men come and count noses in the house. You can distract them and draw their attention away from this room.

You could even flirt a bit; Kurt wouldn't mind."

"I'll do what I can."

Ruti got up and started walking back and forth as if she were modeling clothes, an inviting smile on her face.

"You think this will do?"

Olivia and I laughed. "You should wiggle your hips a little more," Olivia teased.

"Then she is sure to pick up a few officers," I put in.

"Girls, girls, I am a happily married woman, as you know. I cannot let it go too far."

A new party of German soldiers in many trucks drove up to the house the next morning. There were some SS men with them. Olivia and Ruti ran out of the house to meet them and engage the SS men in conversation to give me time to hide. I hid between the two mattresses in the bed and lay still there all day, afraid to breathe. The heavy mattress pressed so hard on me that the circulation was hindered in my hands and feet.

The trucks left that evening. Olivia came in and signalled me to come out. My stomach was giving me trouble. To get to the outhouse I had to pass by the staff people in the front room.

"I need to go to the outhouse," I whispered to Olivia. "I can't stand it any longer."

"Walk boldly past the officers, don't be afraid, these are new ones anyway."

I covered my head and looking to neither left nor right walked out as though this place belonged to me.

Two more days passed. Ruti was now very friendly toward me. According to Olivia she defended me in all the family conversations.

"I must leave you now," Ruti notified us that evening.

"You just got here. Can't you stay another couple of days?" old Mrs. Viliumson was pleading.

"Think of Kurt. He will be out of his mind with worry. Besides in times like this I should be at his side."

There was no disagreement. We embraced as usual and Ruti was off on her bicycle. It was a sad parting. Nobody had much to say.

Events were moving at a feverish pace. The next day the Urkevich family came running over, scared and in a panic. "Great misfortunes," the old man mumbled. "Great misfortunes await us . . . The Germans chasing . . . chasing everybody."

"Take hold of yourself, Adam, talk sense," Mr. Viliumson was shaking Mr. Urkevich, holding on to his shoulders. "The Germans are chasing whom, where, why?"

"Three of them came on a motorcycle and read a paper to us. Yes, a paper. A new law, a command, a directive that everybody in the village must move to Germany. Two hours. Two hours they gave us."

We were stunned and frightened just like the Urkeviches.

"Well, this man is not moving," Mr. Viliumson proclaimed after he recovered. "I was born on this land, my ancestors are buried here, and there will be room enough for me."

"Everything we own is here, too, the land, the house and the livestock. We can't take that to Germany," Mrs. Urkevich lamented.

"I just couldn't part with my red milker," Mrs. Viliumson put in.

"But what will the Reds do to us?" Mr. Urkevich said, leaning on his cane.

"You are too frightened by all this propaganda," Mr. Viliumson replied. "We have nothing to fear from the Reds or anybody else. Besides, they will need people like us to till the soil."

"What do you propose to do?"

"Bunker. We'll excavate a bunker and hide there until the change in power takes place. I know just the place to dig — at the edge of the forest in the hollow. The soil is moist and safe there. It will be easy digging. We can plant some saplings right there to reinforce the roof of the caves. Nobody will notice."

"I know this place, Ferdinand. It will not suit us," Mr. Urkevich argued. "We have a bigger household and more livestock. I know a place, about three kilometers from the highway, where there is a nice little meadow surrounded by thick pine."

"Let it be so," Mr. Viliumson turned to leave. "You go to your place and we will go to ours."

"Could Anna go with you and take our cow?" Mrs. Viliumson pleaded. "You wouldn't mind doing that, would you, Anna? It would ruin the cow to leave her unmilked here."

"Certainly," the Urkeviches replied together. "We will love to have her for company and we'll help each other with the animals."

I nodded in agreement. It was all settled.

No sooner had we had reached the house than three SS men on motorcycles came. They dismounted and came up. We already knew their message — move to Germany, abandon the house within two hours . . . terse, sharp, courteous.

There was no time to lose. We hurriedly prepared food and clothing in individual knotted bundles. After brief embraces I cut across the meadow down to the forest leading "my cow" by the rope. Pretty soon I caught up with the Urkeviches. They were slowly plodding along over the tangled forest paths, driving their stock in front of them. My cow joined their company.

After about five kilometers we came to a little meadow, surrounded by dense forest. Our trek, however, was interrupted for over a day by an intense bombardment of the whole area. We lay flat on the ground as shells from big guns went whistling overhead and exploded with tremendous force all around us. Bombs poured out from planes like seeds from a hole in a sack, and exploded in the distance. The cows, and sheep, after getting used to the new place, grazed peacefully all through the din, crash, and thunder of the bombs.

Miracle of miracles! Not one bomb exploded in our little meadow. I was both frightened and jubilant. I wanted to shout to the planes, "Give it to them, give it to them!"

The bombardment stopped as suddenly as it started. The planes, too, were gone. We continued our flight. I felt very happy. Pretty soon, pretty soon I'll be liberated and free, free as a bird.

Suddenly we were surrounded by German soldiers and a few SS men. They must have been hiding in the thick of the forest during the bombardment. A couple of the SS men ran to us and shouted, "All refugees must go to the river (Dvina). There are boats waiting for you to take you to Germany."

"Yes, sir. That is where we are going. Thank you, sir — Heil . . ."

They clicked their heels, stretched out their arms — "Heil Hitler!" and were off.

We turned around and crossed the meadow. As we reached the forest the bombardment started again. Bombs virtually rained down on us. It looked as though the Reds were firing at every square meter.

Trees were falling splintered and little fires started in many places.

I had no appetite to go to Germany and now saw my chance to make a run for it, taking advantage of the general confusion.

I got up while everyone else was flattened on the ground and lit out as fast as I could back to the Viliumson's farm. I ran all the way and entered the house. The Germans were gone. The house was empty. I ran down the hill to the Viliumsons' bunker. Everybody was safe. Hardly catching my breath, I shouted, "Don't dare put your noses outside. The Germans are driving everybody to the boats."

I was off again to the Urkeviches in the forest but approached them this time from the other side of the village.

I found the Urkevich family where I had left them, still flat on the ground even though the bombardment had ceased some time ago. They told me that the Germans had ordered them to lie flat on the ground until they came for them. There were no Germans in sight.

"If you are waiting for the Germans to return and ship you like cattle to Germany, you are crazy. Let's go deeper into the forest and start digging our bunker," I said. "The livestock should be tied up loosely so they can graze and not wander off."

There was strength and authority in my voice. In the face of their fright, indecision and confusion, I took over and they followed gladly.

About two or three kilometers deeper into the forest, we stopped. We tried up the livestock and started making dugouts. We worked to exhaustion, digging in the ground, cutting timbers and installing them for reinforcements and setting up housekeeping. In two days our refuge was finished. It was a crawl-in affair to hide in and wait out the bombardment. Now we could relax. There were no Germans or anybody else around.

Toward evening another bombardment started. The Reds let go with everything they had. The people in the dugout were shaking with fright, while I felt close to heaven, like on the eve of a big holiday or a forthcoming celebration. I started comforting my friends.

"Don't be frightened," I said. "You can see that not a bomb has fallen here. Why? Because there is not a German around, and the Russians know it. Nobody is shooting from here at the Reds. They have their scouts out and they won't waste ammunition on us."

The logic of my deductions made sense to them and I started believing it myself. We gradually crawled out into the waning daylight. The bombardment though still intense could be heard farther west.

My friends were looking up to me and probably wondering why I was so cheerful while they were concerned about how they would fare under the Reds. That was my secret, which I decided to keep for the time being.

We spent that night in our dugouts. I slept well, better than in the last three years. That constant fear of being discovered was gone.

I was up with the first sunlight and roused the rest of them. The shooting was now farther away and nobody paid any attention to it.

We went to milk the cows. My red one was still lying down and chewing her cud. She gave me a friendly grunt of recognition and got up. I squatted in position to milk her while she swatted flies with her tail.

We drank all the milk we could, but there was just

too much of it and we had no implements to make butter, cream, or cheese. We wasted buckets of milk, pouring it into the ground.

Thus several days passed in relative quiet with neither side making an appearance. Only the far-off shooting reminded us that there was still fighting going on.

12. The Liberation

The shooting behind the forest stopped suddenly. It became unusually quiet. We listened intently to catch an indication of the location of the front. Only the gentle breeze in the leaves could be heard.

We sat listening for over an hour without muttering a word. Only the cry of a bird would occasionally break the silence. We could stand it no longer. I got up and said, "I will go to the village and find out what is going on."

Mrs. Urkevich halted me. "I'd better go. It is safer for an old woman," and she left.

Before long she came running back shouting, "Get up, the Red Army is coming!"

The news seared like a flame. I started running as fast as I could toward the highway. Out of the forest I jumped over a wide ditch and onto the road. There was no mistake: the Reds were here. Some of them were resting on the side of the road, others were marching in both directions. The road was full of military traffic.

"Hurrah! Hurrah!" I shouted. "Liberators, saviors of humanity!"

Some of the soldiers looked at me with wonder and suspicion. I must have looked crazy to them; I probably was.

I turned and ran to the Viliumsons' bunker. They were still there.

"Come out! Come out!" I shouted. "It is all over; the Nazis are gone, the Reds are here!"

We cried and hugged and kissed and congratulated each other for staying alive.

After we calmed down a bit, we collected our belongings and started toward the house. There on the ground by the fence lay a dead Red Army soldier, his hands clutching his chest, eyes open in a fixed stare into space.

We went on to the house. It looked as though there had been a big fight around the house. All the windows were punctured by bullets and the walls and roof showed gaping holes from shell fragments. The roof of the stall was torn off all altogether.

"Oh, what destruction!" Mrs. Viliumson cried as we went into the house. Broken furniture, glass, pottery shards, wilted house plants littered the floor. Shafts of sunlight came through the ceiling.

"We have some work to do," Mr. Viliumson observed as he started pushing things aside with his cane to clear a passage for himself.

We heard a car drive up and I ran out to greet it. I was ready to hug and kiss every Red soldier. The sight, however, stopped me. About half a dozen Red soldiers were approaching the house, guns at the ready.

"Where is the old man?" an officer asked with anger in his voice.

"Mr. Viliumson? He is here. What do you want with Mr. Viliumson?"

"He is a German, isn't he?"

"Yes."

"He killed the soldier there by the fence."

"No, he didn't! He couldn't! He just came from hiding out in the forest."

"Your neighbors said he did. He is a German saboteur."

October, 1977 in Israel

Michelson Family After the War

"No, no, what are you saying!"

Ferdinand Viliumson, leaning on his cane, came out to see what was going on. Two soldiers started to approach him.

"Don't you dare touch him!" I exploded, throwing back my head scarf and letting my black hair fall. For the first time in four years I looked people straight in the eyes and was not hiding my hair.

"I am a Jewess, as you can see. This man, whom you are falsely accusing, hid me out from the Nazi murderers for four years at the risk of his and his family's lives. It is thanks to him that I stand before you alive."

"We shall see if you are telling the truth," the officer said. "Comrade Rabinovich, see if she is Jewish."

A Jewish-looking young man with sergeant's stripes came over and started talking Yiddish to me. I hadn't heard this language since the escape from the death march. I broke down and cried. I told him some of my experiences in Yiddish. A crowd was gathering around us.

"There is no doubt she is telling the truth," Rabinovich turned to the officer. "She says she is probably the only one of more than 30,000 women and children who escaped the Fascist shooting gallery in Rumbuli Forest."

The atmosphere changed. The soldiers started shaking hands with the Viliumsons and me, started asking questions about our ordeal. The officer even promised to recommend the Viliumsons for an award in recognition of their humanity in the face of danger to their own lives.

The news that a Jewish girl was saved from the Rumbuli shootings through all those years of Nazi occupation spread far and wide. I had to tell my story over and over again. For a long time friends, people from the military garrison, from newspapers, and from the Special Commission for Investigation of Nazi atrocities were coming for details of my story.

It was impossible to tell everyone everything. Therefore, I decided to write down all my experiences in the form of notes. Several notebooks were filled. Someday I will have children. Let them read it when they grow up; let them read it and never forget it.

This is how this book came into existence.

13. *Afterword*

It is hard to describe the elation, the state of euphoria, of the handful of Jews who somehow had managed to stay alive when the Russians liberated Riga. Gradually other Jews who had fled to Russia started returning to Riga. Once we assembled in a large room. There were eighty-seven survivors of the men's ghetto and myself from the women's ghetto. One by one each of us spoke, told our experiences, ridding ourselves of accumulated frustrations, and telling of the many miracles that had kept us alive.

After I spoke, it became evident that I was the only one of more than 30,000 people to escape the two *aktionen* (campaigns, extermination drives). The audience surrounded me and bombarded me with questions about their families and relatives; had I seen them, known them, what they had talked about, their actions and conduct during the last days and moments of their lives.

A young man introduced himself as Motia Michelson. He was about 1.75 meters tall, slender and frail, with a typical Jewish elongated face and sad, black eyes.

Motia was one of the eighty-seven survivors of the Riga ghetto. He made good his second escape from the Mezhaparka concentration camp during the last days of the Nazi occupation of Riga. Motia asked if he could walk me home that evening. I agreed. We were married a week later.

We started to pick up the pieces and reconstruct

our lives. We moved into the empty apartment of the Scheinks. Frau Scheink and her husband had fled to Germany in the fall of 1944. They probably still live there.

I found out that a man by the name of Villis Latis had my furniture. He gave it up only after I threatened to inform the authorities and take him to court.

It took little time to reestablish my shop for made-to-order ladies' suits and dresses. Motia took up his electrical engineering profession again.

Olivia's brother Hein who had been inducted into the German army in 1944 as a cook was killed by a shell fragment in the front lines during the German retreat from Latvia that year. Hein's wife, Edith, and her mother were evacuated to Germany.

Kurt was taken by boat to Prussia. He lives now in West Germany. His wife, Ruti, stayed in Riga. She later met her death in an automobile accident.

Olivia passed away like a spent candle as I held her in my arms in 1945. She was delirious for a couple of hours before the end. There she lay in my arms, a bundle of bones held together with skin. The disease had taken its toll. There will not be another such close friend in my life to match this German girl with her deep faith in God and her clear, warm soul.

My dear, kind Pesla suffered for a long time with her many ailments. We helped her as we could. She, like Olivia, died in 1945.

The deaths of Hein and Olivia and the scattering of the rest of the family were very hard on my saviors, the old Viliumsons. They both passed away in 1949 on their farm near Katlakalns. With their demise there was none of their family left in Latvia. This was a great loss to me. Only my memories and eternal gratitude for this life that they saved will remain forever in my mind and heart.

From the Berzinsh family, the son Alfred and my savior, his old mother Emily, both died. The others are alive and well. We meet often.

Sasha and Greta live in Riga. They are my best friends. We, too, meet often, welded together by the harsh experiences of four years of friendship, hardship, and suffering.

* * *

I was requested to report to the K.G.B. Special Commission which was investigating the German atrocities during the war years. They gave me a very friendly reception when I arrived. Very few questions were asked; they let me talk at will while notes were taken. At the end came a question: "How is it that you are still alive?"

I did not understand the question and was confused. "What do you mean why am I still here?" I truly did not understand.

Steel hard blue eyes looked at me intently without emotion, without compassion, and the question was repeated. By now the unspoken meaning penetrated: What had I given the Germans so that they would let me live. I felt my face growing red with anger.

"It took the selfless goodness of some people, some miracles, and my own perseverance to stay alive so that I could stand here now before you and tell my story and the story of tens of thousands who did not survive!" Head held high and eyes blazing, I almost shouted my answer, and damn the consequences. I got up and left. Nobody tried to stop me.

The man who had interrogated me was Latvian. My story contained many instances of brutality by Latvians. I thought that this may have been the cause for his question. Later, however, it became clear what the K.G.B.'s reasoning was: the only way some Jews could have escaped death was that they were in the employ of the Germans. Several people were arrested and were accused of being German spies. After many investigations, these accusations were laid to rest. Even returned prisoners of war from Germany were regarded with suspicion and many of them were sent away for years at hard labor. The few of us who escaped the Nazis could finally resume normal lives.

* * *

My first son, Liova, was born in 1945. We led a relatively quiet life for the next four years. But in 1949 rumors began circulating that all people about whom suspicion of any kind existed would be sent to Siberia. This included politically untrustworthy citizens, the bourgeois, especially big Latvian landowners, and of course, Jews. The talk was that trains were already being assembled, any day now . . .

My husband and I, with our four-year-old boy, were getting ready food, warm clothing, shoes, and trying to adjust our mental state to the inevitable. I was six months pregnant, and my sister-in-law strongly recommended that I have an abortion. I refused. What will be will be.

It turned out that only the rich farmers who had not volunteered to join the collective farms were sent away to Siberia. Again we returned to normal.

* * *

One day when I was shopping in the marketplace I heard a female voice scream, "There she is! There she is!"

Two women were staring at me as though I were a ghost, one pointing a finger at me.

It was Sarah and Neha, my two long lost sisters. We

were in each others' arms, kissing, hugging, crying, and asking questions.

They had taken the last refugee train out of Riga before the Germans came and were evacuated deep into Eastern Russia. There they lived through the whole war in work and deprivation. After the end of the war, they were shipped back to where they came from.

I never thought I would ever find them alive, neither had they thought that I could survive.

*   *   *

On November 3, 1951 in the early evening, there was a loud knock on our apartment door. Two K.G.B. men stood in the hallway with a paper in hand. They entered and announced that Motia was to be arrested. The men searched the apartment, primarily among the books and Motia's papers. They confiscated some of Motia's Yiddish and Hebrew books and all of his handwritten notes. A binder with my handwritten notes on my life and experiences through the four years of Nazi occupation was also taken.

My second son, Dania, was then one year and four months old. For a time the K.G.B. men held Motia in the basement of the K.G.B. building. He was later transferred to the Central Prison where they kept him for a year.

I was called very often to the K.G.B. for interrogation. Time and again I had to retell my life story; how I met Motia, who his friends were, what places we went to, how good a husband he was, had he slandered the Soviet Union, if I knew about his past associations, and on and on . . .

One time I asked my inquisitors, "What is my husband accused of?"

"Don't you know of his crimes?" came the reply.

"Why, he is and was a counterrevolutionary, an enemy of the State and the working people. During our search of your house we found materials that clearly show he was a leader of the Zionist-Revisionist groups, a Fascist and a traitor to the Soviet Union. He gave illegal help to defectors of the Soviet Union and agitated against the State. In one case he knew of a runaway from this country and did not report him."

There was a trial by the infamous Troika, three judges in a closed trial. With the help of false witnesses, Motia was condemned to ten years at hard labor — digging coal in the mines of Vorkuta, above the Arctic Circle in the Russian tundra.

This was what came out at the trial. A person named Spitz left Latvia illegally. A man named Zemet was arrested because he knew of Spitz's flight and failed to report it. Zemet implicated Motia during his interrogation. He said that Motia knew and had helped Spitz flee the country, that Motia was a leader of the Zionist-Revisionist Jewish groups.

I was not permitted to visit Motia. I could only send him parcels of food and clothing and that not too often.

The prison administration did not trust Motia to work as an electrical engineer, so he was assigned to the coal mines. The harsh climate, the unusually hard labor and poor food broke Motia's health. He contracted jaundice. After that they transferred him to office work.

Shortly before death, Stalin issued orders to rid the Soviet Union of "all suspicious Jews." I was certain that this included me, for I was the wife of a "political criminal." This meant that I would be sent away. To ease my burden, my brother-in-law and sister suggested that they adopt my older son, Liova. For days on end we went from office to office to bring about the adoption. Because we lacked one or another document the adoption never came about. Stalin's death solved this problem — the adoption proceedings were dropped. I stayed in Riga.

* * *

In August 1953 after Stalin's death, I finally received permission to visit Motia. I hardly recognized him. He looked like a living corpse, parchment-yellow skin drawn over his bones, the big sad eyes devoid of hope.

Motia was "technically" freed in the general amnesty that followed Stalin's death. However, they did not free him then. Instead, they sent him to Kostroma. Only in 1956, three years after Stalin's death, during the Khrushchev era, was Motia "rehabilitated." In plain language, all accusations against him were dropped, and he was a free man. He had been at hard labor for a total of five and a half years.

My husband was a broken man, failing in health, when he came home. He dedicated the rest of his life to collecting documents, eyewitness accounts, and taking notes of the fate of the Jewish people who perished during the Nazi occupation.

My notes of my own experiences that had been confiscated by the K.G.B. were never returned. Motia forced me to write them again so that our children and perhaps others would know how it was and maybe prevent it from happening again. These notes were completed in 1966 and were the basis for this book.

* * *

Motia loved Israel with his mind, his heart, and his soul. He saw Israel as the only hope for the survival of the Jewish nation. He brought up our two sons in this spirit. Alas, his cherished wish to see Israel did not come true. He was in poor health when he came back from *Lager*. He died in 1966 of a heart attack.

My son, Liova, his wife and her parents, left for Israel in June, 1971. My second son, Dania, my sister Sarah, and I followed Liova on the strength of his exit permit (to keep families together) and arrived in Israel on December 29, 1971.

* * *

Both my sons graduated from the Moscow Technical University (M.T.U.), Liova in Physics and Dania in Mathematics.

We are now all here in Israel. Liova and his family live in Haifa. He made his Ph.D. in the Technion and works temporarily as a physics instructor. His ambition is to go into physics research. Dania and his family are in Tel Aviv. He teaches mathematics at the University of Tel Aviv and will shortly get his Ph.D in the subject.

My sister Sarah and I live in a new two-bedroom apartment in Haifa. At last I can say I have found peace of soul, to be among my own. Only my conscience never lets me rest, as is true with the other survivors of the Holocaust. Why am I alive and all my friends are gone? We will have to live with that — there is no answer; there will always be hurt deep inside me whenever I think of it.

As for Israel, I feel at home as I have never felt anywhere else. To me, this is truly the promised land, a land I can be proud of and proudly give my life for. A place where one can think and speak freely, where one is free of the constant fear of arrest and search, where a policeman or a functionary is a servant, not an overlord. I came home, a good home, a home at last.

Frida Michelson